Hustle Harder

How to Dominate the Game and Crush
Your Competition

Akshat Mishra
Vinit Saraogi

Copyright © 2023 by Akshat Mishra and Vinit Saraogi.

All rights reserved. No part of this book may be reproduced or transmitted in any form or by any means, electronic or mechanical, including photocopying, recording, or by any information storage and retrieval system, without permission in writing from the author.

The information contained in this book is for general information purposes only. The author makes no representations or warranties of any kind, express or implied, about the completeness, accuracy, reliability, suitability, or availability with respect to the book or the information, products, services, or related graphics contained in the book for any purpose. Any reliance you place on such information is therefore strictly at your own risk.

In no event will the author be liable for any loss or damage including without limitation, indirect or consequential loss or damage, or any loss or damage whatsoever arising from loss of data or profits arising out of, or in connection with, the use of this book.

Every effort has been made to ensure that the information contained in this book is accurate and up-to-date. However, the author makes no guarantee that the information provided in this book is correct, complete, or current at all times.

Thank you for choosing to read this book. Your support and feedback are greatly appreciated.

Dear Hustler,

This book is dedicated to all the hustlers out there, who wake up every day with a burning desire to chase their dreams and achieve greatness.

To my parents, who taught me the value of hard work and never gave up on me, even when I failed.

To my mentors, who guided me through the ups and downs of my journey, and showed me what it means to be a true hustler.

To my friends, who supported me and cheered me on when I needed it most, and reminded me to never give up.

And most importantly, to my readers, who have taken the time to pick up this book and invest in themselves. Remember, the hustle is not just about making money or achieving fame, it's about the journey of self-discovery and personal growth. Keep pushing yourself, keep hustling harder, and never stop believing in yourself.

This book is for you.

Sincerely,
Akshat Mishra

Content

1. **Introduction: The Hustler Mindset**
   - What it takes to be a successful entrepreneur
   - The importance of hard work, perseverance, and resilience
   - How to develop a winning mindset
2. **Finding Your Niche**
   - Identifying your strengths and passions
   - Conducting market research to find a profitable niche
   - Choosing a business model that fits your goals and personality
3. **Building Your Brand**
   - Creating a unique and memorable brand identity
   - Developing a strong value proposition and messaging
   - Leveraging social media and other marketing channels to build a following
4. **Developing a Winning Strategy**
   - Setting clear goals and objectives
   - Conducting a SWOT analysis to identify opportunities and threats
   - Creating a roadmap to success and measuring progress along the way
5. **Hustling for Funding**
   - Understanding the different types of funding available
   - Creating a solid business plan and pitch
   - Networking and building relationships with investors

6. **Building Your Dream Team**
   - Identifying the key roles and skills needed for your business
   - Hiring, training, and managing employees and contractors
   - Fostering a culture of innovation, collaboration, and accountability
7. **Scaling Up**
   - Understanding the challenges and opportunities of scaling your business
   - Developing systems and processes to streamline operations
   - Expanding your product/service offerings and markets
8. **Crushing Your Competition**
   - Staying ahead of the game by innovating and adapting
   - Building a loyal customer base and reputation
   - Maintaining a competitive edge through continuous learning and improvement
9. **Maintaining Work-Life Balance**
   - Avoiding burnout and managing stress
   - Prioritizing self-care and personal growth
   - Creating a fulfilling and sustainable lifestyle as an entrepreneur
10. **Conclusion: The Hustle Never Ends**
    - Recap of key lessons and takeaways
    - Encouragement to keep hustling and pursuing your dreams
    - Final thoughts and inspiration to keep pushing forward.

Preface
Welcome to the Game

Welcome to the game of life, where success is not guaranteed, and failure is always lurking around the corner. It takes a special kind of mindset to rise to the top, a mindset that I call the hustler mindset. In this book, I will share with you the principles and strategies that I have learned throughout my journey, from struggling to make ends meet to dominating the game.

Before we begin, I want to make it clear that this book is not a magic solution that will guarantee you success overnight. It's a guide that will equip you with the tools and mindset necessary to crush your competition and achieve your goals. It's up to you to put in the work, to hustle harder than anyone else, and never give up on your dreams.

Throughout the pages of this book, you'll discover the power of a positive mindset, the importance of hard work and perseverance, and the value of strategic thinking. You'll learn how to overcome obstacles, how to turn failures into opportunities, and how to stay motivated in the face of adversity.

I hope this book inspires you to take action, to embrace the hustle, and to dominate the game. Remember, the journey to success is not easy, but it's worth it. So let's get started and hustle harder than ever before!

Acknowledgment

I would like to express my gratitude to all those who have supported me throughout the journey of writing this book. Firstly, I would like to thank my family for their unwavering support and encouragement. They have always been my biggest cheerleaders and provided me with the motivation to keep pushing through any obstacles.

I also want to thank my close friends and colleagues who have always believed in me and provided me with constructive feedback throughout the writing process.

A special thanks to my editor and publisher for their expertise and guidance in bringing this book to life. Their invaluable insights and suggestions have truly elevated the quality of the final product.

I would also like to extend my appreciation to all the individuals who have inspired me and taught me the importance of the hustler mindset. From successful entrepreneurs to legendary athletes, your stories have been a constant source of motivation for me.

Finally, I would like to express my gratitude to the readers who have chosen to pick up this book. It is my hope that the ideas and insights presented here will help you to cultivate the hustler mindset and achieve your own definition of success.

"If you want to conquer fear, don't sit home and think about it. Go out and get busy.."
— **Dale Carnegie**

Chapter 1: Introduction: The Hustler Mindset

I. **Introduction**
- Definition of a successful entrepreneur
- Importance of understanding what it takes to be successful

II. **Key Qualities of Successful Entrepreneurs**
- Passion and motivation
- Resilience and perseverance
- Creativity and innovation
- Strong work ethic
- Adaptability and flexibility
- Risk-taking and courage
- Resourcefulness and problem-solving skills
- Emotional intelligence and strong interpersonal skills

III. **Building Your Brand**
- Business acumen and financial literacy
- Marketing and sales skills
- Strategic thinking and planning
- Leadership and team management
- Networking and collaboration
- Continuous learning and self-improvement

IV. **Real-life Examples of Successful Entrepreneurs**
- Case studies of successful entrepreneurs and their journeys
- Lessons learned from their successes and failures

V. **Conclusion**
- Recap of key points
- Encouragement to develop and cultivate the necessary qualities, skills, and knowledge for success in entrepreneurship.

Chapter 1: Introduction: The Hustler Mindset

I. Introduction

Being a successful entrepreneur is a dream of many, but few manage to achieve it. What does it take to be a successful entrepreneur? In this chapter, we will define what it means to be a successful entrepreneur and discuss the importance of understanding what it takes to be successful.

Definition of a successful entrepreneur:

Before we discuss what it takes to be a successful entrepreneur, it is essential to define what we mean by a successful entrepreneur. A successful entrepreneur is someone who has started a business venture and has been able to turn it into a profitable and sustainable enterprise. However, being a successful entrepreneur is more than just making a profit. A successful entrepreneur is someone who has created something valuable that has made a positive impact on the world.

Importance of understanding what it takes to be successful:

To become a successful entrepreneur, you need to have a clear understanding of what it takes to be successful. This understanding will help you set realistic goals, develop a solid business plan, and make the necessary decisions to move your business forward.

Understanding what it takes to be successful means knowing your strengths and weaknesses, having a clear vision of your goals, and having the ability to take calculated risks. It also means having the right mindset, being resilient, and being willing to put in the hard work required to achieve success.

In the following sections of this chapter, we will explore these essential qualities and skills in more detail, giving you a comprehensive understanding of what it takes to be a successful entrepreneur.

II. Key Qualities of Successful Entrepreneurs

Becoming a successful entrepreneur requires more than just a good business idea. It takes a certain set of qualities and characteristics that are essential to achieving your goals and building a thriving business. Here are some of the key qualities that successful entrepreneurs possess:

Passion and motivation: Passion is what drives many entrepreneurs to start their own business. It's the fuel that keeps them going when the going gets tough. Passion for your business idea is important because it will help you stay focused on your goals and give you the energy you need to overcome challenges and obstacles.

Resilience and perseverance: Starting a business is not an easy task, and there will be times when things don't go as planned. Successful entrepreneurs are resilient and are able to bounce back from setbacks. They have the ability to persevere in the face of adversity and keep moving forward.

Creativity and innovation: Successful entrepreneurs are creative thinkers who are always looking for new and innovative ways to solve problems and meet the needs of their customers. They are not afraid to take risks and try new things.

Strong work ethic: Entrepreneurship requires hard work and dedication. Successful entrepreneurs have a strong work ethic and are willing to put in the time and effort needed to make their business a success.

Adaptability and flexibility: Business environments are constantly changing, and successful entrepreneurs are able to adapt to these changes and adjust their strategies accordingly. They are also flexible and open-minded, which allows them to pivot and change direction when necessary.

Risk-taking and courage: Starting a business involves taking risks, and successful entrepreneurs are not afraid to take calculated risks in order to achieve their goals. They also have the courage to make difficult decisions and take action when needed.

Resourcefulness and problem-solving skills: Entrepreneurship requires resourcefulness and the ability to solve problems. Successful entrepreneurs are able to find creative solutions to problems and are not afraid to seek help and advice when needed.

Emotional intelligence and strong interpersonal skills: Entrepreneurship is all about building relationships with customers, employees, and business partners. Successful entrepreneurs have strong emotional intelligence and are able to build and maintain positive relationships with others. They also have strong interpersonal skills that allow them to communicate effectively and build trust.

In conclusion, successful entrepreneurship requires a combination of these key qualities. While some of these qualities may come naturally to some individuals, others can be developed over time with practice and hard work. By cultivating these qualities and incorporating them into your daily life, you can increase your chances of success as an entrepreneur.

III. Skills and Knowledge Required for Entrepreneurship

To be a successful entrepreneur, you need a specific set of skills and knowledge. These skills and knowledge are not only limited to business but also require emotional intelligence, creativity, and leadership. Here are some of the critical skills and knowledge areas that are necessary for entrepreneurship:

Business acumen and financial literacy:

To be a successful entrepreneur, you must have a solid understanding of business operations and finances. You should have a good understanding of accounting, financial statements, and cash flow. You must know how to manage costs, handle financial risks, and generate profits. If you don't have a background in business or finance, you should consider taking some courses to improve your knowledge.

Marketing and sales skills:

Marketing and sales skills are essential for any entrepreneur. You should know how to create a marketing strategy, identify your target market, and promote your products or services effectively. You should have excellent communication skills and be able to persuade customers to buy your products or services. You should also know how to build strong relationships with customers and retain them over time.

Strategic thinking and planning:

As an entrepreneur, you need to be able to think strategically and plan for the future. You must be able to identify opportunities and threats in the market and adjust your business accordingly. You should have a clear understanding of your business goals and create a roadmap to achieve them. You should be able to anticipate challenges and risks and plan for contingencies.

Leadership and team management:
Entrepreneurship requires excellent leadership and team management skills. You should be able to inspire and motivate your team to work towards your business goals. You should be able to delegate tasks effectively and create a culture of collaboration and innovation. You should also know how to manage conflicts and build strong relationships with your team members.

Networking and collaboration:
Networking and collaboration are critical for any entrepreneur. You should be able to build strong relationships with other entrepreneurs, investors, and industry experts. You should be able to seek advice and support when needed and provide the same to others. You should be able to collaborate with other businesses and individuals to create new opportunities.

Continuous learning and self-improvement:
Entrepreneurship is a journey of continuous learning and self-improvement. You should always be willing to learn new skills and knowledge to improve your business. You should attend conferences, read books and articles, and take courses to keep up with the latest trends in your industry. You should also be willing to seek feedback and work on improving your weaknesses.

In conclusion, entrepreneurship requires a specific set of skills and knowledge. You should have a solid understanding of business operations and finances, marketing and sales skills, strategic thinking and planning, leadership and team management, networking and collaboration, and continuous learning and self-improvement. By mastering these skills and knowledge areas, you can increase your chances of success as an entrepreneur.

IV. Real-life Examples of Successful Entrepreneurs

One of the best ways to learn about entrepreneurship is to study the lives and businesses of successful entrepreneurs. By understanding their journeys and the challenges they faced, we can learn valuable lessons and insights that can help us on our own entrepreneurial paths. Here are some real-life examples of successful entrepreneurs and the lessons we can learn from them:

Jeff Bezos, Founder of **Amazon**: Jeff Bezos is one of the most successful entrepreneurs of our time, having built Amazon from a small online bookstore to a global e-commerce giant. One of the key lessons we can learn from Bezos is the importance of customer obsession. From the beginning, Bezos was committed to creating a company that focused on the needs and desires of its customers, even if it meant taking risks and making bold moves. This customer-centric approach has been a major factor in Amazon's success.

Elon Musk, CEO of **Tesla** and **SpaceX**: Elon Musk is a serial entrepreneur who has founded several successful companies, including Tesla and SpaceX. Musk is known for his visionary thinking and his willingness to take on big challenges. One of the lessons we can learn from Musk is the importance of thinking big and being willing to take risks. Musk has often pursued ambitious goals that many people thought were impossible, but he has been able to achieve them through hard work, determination, and a willingness to fail and learn from his mistakes.

Sara Blakely, Founder of **Spanx:** Sara Blakely is the founder of Spanx, a company that makes slimming undergarments for women.

Blakely started the company with just $5,000 and turned it into a multi-million-dollar business. One of the lessons we can learn from Blakely is the importance of persistence and resilience. Blakely faced numerous rejections and setbacks when she was starting out, but she refused to give up on her vision. She also believes in the power of failure and encourages her team to embrace mistakes as opportunities to learn and grow.

Mark Zuckerberg, Co-founder of **Facebook:** Mark Zuckerberg is the co-founder of Facebook, the largest social media platform in the world. One of the lessons we can learn from Zuckerberg is the importance of innovation and creativity. Zuckerberg has always been focused on creating new and innovative products that can change the way people connect and share information. He has also been willing to pivot and adapt his strategy as needed, which has allowed Facebook to remain a dominant force in the tech industry.

Oprah Winfrey, Media Mogul and Philanthropist: Oprah Winfrey is a media mogul and philanthropist who has built an empire around her brand. One of the lessons we can learn from Oprah is the importance of authenticity and staying true to your values. Oprah has always been open and honest about her struggles and has used her platform to inspire and empower others. She has also been a generous philanthropist, using her wealth and influence to support causes she believes in.

In conclusion, becoming a successful entrepreneur requires a combination of skills, knowledge, and qualities. Entrepreneurs need to have a strong work ethic, be adaptable and flexible, take risks, and have strong interpersonal skills.

They also need to have the skills and knowledge required to start and run a successful business, including business acumen, financial literacy, marketing and sales skills, and strategic thinking. By studying the lives and businesses of successful entrepreneurs, we can learn valuable lessons and insights that can help us on our own entrepreneurial journeys.

V. Conclusion

In this chapter, we have discussed what it takes to be a successful entrepreneur. We have covered the key qualities that successful entrepreneurs possess, including passion, resilience, creativity, a strong work ethic, adaptability, risk-taking, resourcefulness, emotional intelligence, and strong interpersonal skills. We have also discussed the skills and knowledge required for entrepreneurship, including business acumen and financial literacy, marketing and sales skills, strategic thinking and planning, leadership and team management, networking and collaboration, and continuous learning and self-improvement.

To truly succeed as an entrepreneur, it's not enough to just possess these qualities, skills, and knowledge - they must be developed and cultivated over time. This requires a commitment to personal growth and a willingness to learn from both successes and failures. Successful entrepreneurs are lifelong learners who are always looking for ways to improve themselves and their businesses.

To drive home the importance of these qualities, skills, and knowledge, we have also explored real-life examples of successful entrepreneurs and their journeys.

Through case studies, we have seen how these entrepreneurs have overcome obstacles, adapted to changing market conditions, and ultimately achieved success through their determination and hard work.

In conclusion, becoming a successful entrepreneur requires a combination of innate qualities, developed skills, and acquired knowledge. By understanding what it takes to be successful and committing to personal growth, aspiring entrepreneurs can position themselves for success in their chosen fields. So, embrace the hustle mentality, develop your skills and knowledge, and always be willing to learn and grow - with dedication and hard work, you too can dominate the game and crush your competition.

"The only place where success comes before work is in the dictionary."

- Vidal Sassoon

Chapter 2: Finding Your Niche

I. **Introduction**
- Importance of finding your niche in entrepreneurship
- Overview of the chapter

II. **Understanding Niche Markets**
- Definition of niche markets
- Benefits of targeting a niche market
- Examples of successful niche businesses

III. **Identifying Your Strengths and Passions**
- Assessing your skills and interests
- Finding overlap between your skills and market opportunities
- Researching potential niches

IV. **Evaluating Market Demand and Competition**
- Conducting market research
- Analyzing market trends and consumer behavior
- Identifying competitors and their strengths and weaknesses

V. **Creating Your Unique Value Proposition**
- Defining your brand and positioning
- Crafting a unique value proposition
- Identifying your target audience

VI. **Testing and Refining Your Niche**
- Launching a pilot test
- Gathering customer feedback
- Refining your product or service offering

VII. Scaling Your Niche Business
- Strategies for growth and expansion
- Developing systems and processes
- Building a strong team

VIII. Case Studies of Successful Niche Businesses
- Analysis of successful niche businesses and their strategies
- Lessons learned from their experiences

IX. Conclusion
- Recap of key points
- Encouragement to find and pursue a niche market in entrepreneurship.

Chapter 2: Finding Your Niche

Chapter 2 is all about finding your niche in entrepreneurship. While starting a business can be exciting, it's important to identify your niche in order to stand out from the competition and succeed in the long run. This chapter will provide an overview of the importance of finding your niche and offer guidance on how to identify your strengths and passions in order to hone in on a specific area of focus. Whether you're starting a new business or looking to pivot an existing one, this chapter will help you discover your niche and take your entrepreneurial journey to the next level. So let's dive in and explore the world of niche entrepreneurship!

I. Introduction

Finding your niche is one of the most important steps in entrepreneurship. It's the process of identifying the specific area or market that you want to focus on, and where you believe you can provide value and stand out from the competition.

Identifying your niche is crucial for several reasons. First, it allows you to tailor your products or services to a specific audience, making it easier to attract and retain customers. Second, it helps you differentiate yourself from the competition, as you can provide a unique value proposition that sets you apart. Finally, it enables you to establish yourself as an expert in your niche, building credibility and trust with your audience.

However, finding your niche can be challenging, especially if you're not sure where to start. It requires a deep understanding of yourself, your strengths, and your passions, as well as market research and analysis to identify gaps and opportunities. In this chapter, we will explore the process of finding your niche in detail, including the importance of identifying your strengths and passions, conducting market research, and evaluating potential opportunities. We'll also provide practical tips and strategies to help you find your niche and set yourself up for success in entrepreneurship.

II. **Understanding Niche Markets In today's highly** competitive business world, it is crucial to find a way to stand out from the crowd. One of the most effective ways to do this is by identifying and targeting a niche market. In this section, we will define what a niche market is, discuss the benefits of targeting a niche market, and provide examples of successful niche businesses.

A. **Definition of Niche Markets**:

A niche market is a smaller, more specialized subset of a larger market that has unique needs, preferences, or characteristics. Niche markets can be defined by various factors, including demographics, geography, psychographics, behavior, and lifestyle. For example, a niche market could be pet owners who are interested in eco-friendly and sustainable pet products. Another example could be a specific geographic region with a high demand for a particular type of cuisine. The key to identifying a niche market is to look for an unmet need or gap in the market that can be filled with a unique product or service.

B. **Benefits of Targeting a Niche Market**:

Targeting a niche market offers several benefits for entrepreneurs. Some of these benefits include:

Less Competition:

By targeting a niche market, you are focusing on a smaller subset of the market, which means less competition. This can be an advantage, especially for small businesses or startups that may not have the resources to compete with larger, more established companies in a broader market.

Increased Customer Loyalty:

When you cater to a niche market, you are providing a solution to a specific problem or need that is not being met by larger companies. This can result in increased customer loyalty and repeat business, as customers are more likely to stick with a company that caters to their unique needs and preferences.

Higher Profit Margins:

Since niche markets are often underserved, they are willing to pay a premium for products or services that cater to their specific needs. This means that businesses targeting niche markets can often charge higher prices and enjoy higher profit margins.

C. **Examples of Successful Niche Businesses**

There are countless examples of successful niche businesses that have capitalized on the benefits of targeting a niche market. Here are a few examples:

Lush Cosmetics:

Lush is a cosmetics company that specializes in handmade, natural and environmentally friendly products. They have targeted a niche market of environmentally conscious consumers who are looking for alternatives to traditional cosmetics that may contain harmful chemicals.

Warby Parker:
Warby Parker is an eyewear company that offers stylish and affordable glasses and sunglasses. They have targeted a niche market of budget-conscious consumers who are looking for trendy eyewear that won't break the bank.

Dollar Shave Club:
Dollar Shave Club is a subscription-based razor and personal grooming company. They have targeted a niche market of men who are looking for affordable, high-quality razors without the hassle of going to the store.

These are just a few examples of successful niche businesses that have identified a specific market segment and tailored their products and services to meet their unique needs.

In conclusion, targeting a niche market can be a powerful strategy for entrepreneurs looking to stand out in a crowded marketplace. By identifying an unmet need or gap in the market and providing a unique solution, businesses can enjoy the benefits of less competition, increased customer loyalty, and higher profit margins.

III. Identifying Your Strengths and Passions

Identifying your strengths and passions is a crucial step in finding your niche. It involves assessing your skills and interests, finding the overlap between your skills and market opportunities, and researching potential niches. Let's take a closer look at each of these steps.

Assessing your skills and interests:
The first step in identifying your strengths and passions is to assess your skills and interests. Make a list of everything you're good at and enjoy doing, even if it doesn't seem relevant to entrepreneurship. This can include hobbies, volunteer work, past jobs, and other experiences.

Next, take a closer look at each item on your list and identify the skills you used to achieve success in that area. For example, if you're a skilled public speaker, you may have strong communication, presentation, and persuasion skills.

Finding overlap between your skills and market opportunities
Once you've identified your skills, the next step is to find an overlap between your skills and market opportunities. Start by researching industries and markets that align with your interests and skills. Look for areas where you can add value or solve a problem.

For example, if you have a background in graphic design and are passionate about sustainable living, you may consider starting a business that offers eco-friendly design services. This would allow you to use your design skills to help companies create sustainable marketing materials.

Researching potential niches:
After identifying potential markets that align with your skills and interests, the next step is to research potential niches within those markets. This involves looking for gaps in the market or areas where there's room for innovation.

Start by conducting market research to identify potential customers and competitors. Look for trends and patterns in the market to identify potential opportunities. Talk to people in your target market to understand their needs and pain points.

For example, if you're interested in the fitness industry, you may identify a gap in the market for affordable and convenient workout gear. By conducting market research and talking to potential customers, you may discover an opportunity to start a business that offers affordable, high-quality workout gear that can be delivered to customers' homes.

Conclusion

Identifying your strengths and passions is a crucial step in finding your niche. It involves assessing your skills and interests, finding the overlap between your skills and market opportunities, and researching potential niches. By taking the time to identify your strengths and passions and researching potential niches, you'll be better equipped to find a profitable and fulfilling niche in entrepreneurship.

IV. **Evaluating Market Demand and Competition**

When it comes to identifying a niche market, evaluating market demand and competition is a crucial step in the process. This involves conducting market research, analyzing market trends and consumer behavior, and identifying competitors and their strengths and weaknesses.

Conducting Market Research:

Market research involves gathering information about potential customers and their needs, as well as information about competitors and market trends. There are many different methods of conducting market research, such as surveys, focus groups, and online analytics tools.

Surveys can be a useful tool for gathering information about customer preferences and needs. Surveys can be conducted online, through email, or in person. It is important to design the survey questions carefully to ensure that they provide useful information.

Focus groups can be helpful in gaining more detailed insights into customer behavior and preferences. A focus group is a small group of people who are asked to discuss a specific product or service. The insights gained from focus groups can be used to refine product or service offerings to better meet customer needs.

Online analytics tools can be used to gather information about website traffic, social media engagement, and other online metrics. This information can be used to gain insights into customer behavior and preferences.

Analyzing Market Trends and Consumer Behavior:

Market trends and consumer behavior are constantly evolving, and it is important to stay up-to-date with these changes. One way to do this is to analyze industry reports and publications to gain insights into emerging trends and consumer preferences.

Another way to analyze market trends and consumer behavior is to monitor social media platforms and other online forums. By analyzing social media conversations and other online discussions, entrepreneurs can gain insights into what customers are saying about their products or services, as well as what they like and dislike about them.

Identifying Competitors and Their Strengths and Weaknesses:

Identifying competitors and their strengths and weaknesses is an important step in evaluating market demand and competition. This can be done through a variety of methods, such as online research and competitive analysis.

Online research involves looking at competitors' websites, social media profiles, and other online platforms to gain insights into their products and services. This information can be used to identify potential gaps in the market that the entrepreneur can exploit.

Competitive analysis involves analyzing competitors' products and services in more detail. This can be done by purchasing competitors' products or services and analyzing them, or by conducting a SWOT analysis (strengths, weaknesses, opportunities, threats) of the competitor.

By conducting a thorough evaluation of market demand and competition, entrepreneurs can identify potential niche markets that are not being served by competitors. This can help to ensure the success of the entrepreneur's business by focusing on a specific target market that has a strong demand for the products or services being offered.

V. Creating Your Unique Value Proposition

Creating a unique value proposition is the key to stand out in the crowded market and succeed in your niche. A value proposition is a statement that explains what makes your product or service unique and valuable for the target audience. It describes the benefits that your customers will receive and how your product or service can solve their problems better than your competitors.

Defining your brand and positioning:

The first step in creating your unique value proposition is to define your brand and positioning. Branding is about creating a unique identity for your business that sets it apart from your competitors. It is not just about your logo and colors but also about the personality and values of your business.

Your brand should reflect the unique characteristics of your business, such as your mission, vision, and core values. It should also resonate with your target audience and communicate the benefits of your product or service.

Positioning is about how you want your business to be perceived in the market. It is the unique space that your business occupies in the minds of your target audience. To define your positioning, you need to analyze your competitors, identify their strengths and weaknesses, and find a gap that you can fill with your unique value proposition.

Crafting a unique value proposition:

Crafting a unique value proposition is the next step in creating your niche business. Your value proposition should communicate the unique benefits of your product or service to your target audience. It should be clear, concise, and easy to understand.

To create a value proposition, you need to answer the following questions:

- What problem does your product or service solve?
- What are the benefits of your product or service?
- What makes your product or service unique?
- Why should your target audience choose your product or service over your competitors?

Your value proposition should be based on your strengths and your target audience's needs. It should also be aligned with your branding and positioning.

Identifying your target audience:

Identifying your target audience is another critical aspect of creating your unique value proposition. You need to understand who your ideal customer is, what their needs are, and how your product or service can solve their problems better than your competitors.

To identify your target audience, you can use demographic and psychographic data. Demographic data includes age, gender, income, education, and location, while psychographic data includes values, interests, and personality traits.

By understanding your target audience, you can create a value proposition that resonates with them and communicates the benefits of your product or service in a way that they can relate to.

In conclusion, creating a unique value proposition is crucial to succeed in your niche business. It requires defining your brand and positioning, crafting a clear and concise value proposition, and identifying your target audience's needs. By doing so, you can stand out in the crowded market and attract loyal customers who appreciate the unique benefits of your product or service.

VI. Testing and Refining Your Niche

Congratulations! You have made it to the final step in finding your niche - testing and refining your niche. At this point, you have identified your passions and skills, evaluated market demand and competition, and created a unique value proposition. Now it's time to see how your niche fits into the real world.

Launching a Pilot Test:

Before fully committing to your niche, it's important to test the waters first. This is where a pilot test comes in. A pilot test is a small-scale experiment or trial of your product or service to a limited audience to evaluate its performance and gather feedback. The purpose of a pilot test is to identify potential problems, refine your product or service offering, and gain valuable insights into your target audience's preferences and behavior.

When launching a pilot test, it's important to set specific goals and objectives. What do you want to achieve with the pilot test? What metrics will you use to measure success? How long will the pilot test run? These are all important questions to consider before launching your pilot test.

Gathering Customer Feedback:

During the pilot test, it's crucial to gather customer feedback. This can be done through surveys, interviews, or focus groups. The feedback you receive from your target audience will provide valuable insights into what works and what needs improvement.

When gathering feedback, it's important to keep an open mind and take constructive criticism. Use the feedback to refine your product or service offering and make it even better. Remember, your target audience is the key to the success of your niche.

Refining Your Product or Service Offering

Based on the feedback you receive from your target audience, refine your product or service offering. This could involve making changes to your product or service, adjusting your pricing strategy, or targeting a different audience. The goal is to make your niche as appealing and successful as possible.

When refining your niche, it's important to stay true to your unique value proposition. Don't compromise your brand identity or what sets you apart from the competition. Instead, use the feedback you receive to enhance your niche and make it even more attractive to your target audience.

Conclusion

Finding your niche is a crucial step in entrepreneurship. It allows you to stand out from the competition and create a unique value proposition.

By understanding niche markets, identifying your strengths and passions, evaluating market demand and competition, creating a unique value proposition, and testing and refining your niche, you can successfully dominate the game and crush your competition. Remember, finding your niche is not a one-time event - it's an ongoing process that requires constant evaluation and refinement. With the right mindset and strategy, you can build a successful and profitable niche business.

VII. Scaling Your Niche Business

In the previous sections of this chapter, we have discussed how to identify your niche market, evaluate its demand and competition, and create a unique value proposition for your brand. Now that you have a solid understanding of your niche market and have tested your product or service offering, it's time to focus on scaling your niche business. Scaling a business refers to the process of expanding its operations to meet the growing demands of the market. It involves developing strategies for growth and expansion, building systems and processes, and hiring the right team to support your business. In this section, we will discuss each of these aspects in detail.

I. **Strategies for Growth and Expansion:** Once you have successfully tested your niche business, it's time to start thinking about how to expand and grow it. Here are some strategies you can consider:

1. **Diversification:** One way to grow your niche business is by diversifying your product or service offerings. This can involve expanding into related markets or introducing new products or services that complement your existing offering. For example, if you run a niche bakery that specializes in gluten-free pastries, you could consider diversifying your offerings to include vegan and paleo-friendly options.
2. **Geographic expansion:** Another way to scale your niche business is by expanding your reach geographically. This can involve opening new locations or entering new markets that have a similar customer profile to your existing market. For example, if you run a niche boutique that caters to a specific demographic, you could consider opening a new store in a different city that has a similar customer base.
3. **Strategic partnerships:** Collaborating with other businesses can also help you expand your niche business. This can involve partnering with complementary businesses to offer bundled products or services or working with influencers to promote your brand to their audience.

II. **Developing Systems and Processes:** As your niche business grows, it becomes essential to develop systems and processes that can support its operations. This involves creating a streamlined workflow that can handle increased demand while maintaining quality and efficiency.

1. **Automation:** One way to develop systems and processes is by automating repetitive tasks such as order processing, inventory management, and customer support. This can help free up time and resources, allowing you to focus on strategic growth.
2. **Standardization:** Standardizing your processes can also help improve efficiency and consistency. This involves creating clear guidelines and procedures for tasks such as product development, marketing, and customer service.

III. **Building a Strong Team:** Finally, as you scale your niche business, it becomes critical to build a strong team that can support your growth. This involves hiring employees who share your vision and values and can help you achieve your goals.

1. **Hiring for culture fit:** When hiring, it's essential to look for candidates who share your company's values and culture. This can help ensure that everyone is working towards the same goal and is committed to the success of the business.
2. **Training and development:** Investing in your employees' training and development can also help you build a strong team. This involves providing ongoing training and support to help them grow and develop their skills.

In conclusion, scaling your niche business requires a strategic approach that involves diversification, geographic expansion, and strategic partnerships. It also involves developing systems and processes to support your operations and building a strong team that shares your vision and values. By following these strategies, you can take your niche business to the next level and dominate the game.

VIII. Case Studies of Successful Niche Businesses

When it comes to finding your niche, looking at successful businesses and the strategies they employed can provide valuable insights and inspiration. In this section, we will examine some case studies of successful niche businesses and identify the lessons that can be learned from their experiences.

Warby Parker:

Warby Parker is an American online retailer of prescription glasses and sunglasses. Founded in 2010, the company disrupted the traditional eyewear industry by offering stylish, high-quality glasses at affordable prices.

What set Warby Parker apart was its unique business model. The company designed its own glasses, cutting out the middlemen and selling directly to consumers online. By doing so, they were able to offer glasses at a fraction of the cost of traditional retailers.

Another factor in Warby Parker's success was its focus on social responsibility. For every pair of glasses sold, the company donated a pair to someone in need. This gave customers an added incentive to choose Warby Parker over their competitors.

The lesson to be learned from Warby Parker's success is that a unique business model and a focus on social responsibility can set a business apart from its competitor

Dollar Shave Club:

Dollar Shave Club is a California-based company that offers subscription-based razor and personal grooming products. Founded in 2011, the company quickly gained a following with its humorous marketing campaigns and affordable, high-quality products.

What made Dollar Shave Club successful was its subscription-based business model. Customers could sign up for a monthly subscription and receive a regular supply of razors and grooming products delivered right to their door. By doing so, the company was able to build a loyal customer base and generate a steady stream of recurring revenue.

Dollar Shave Club's success also came from its focus on customer experience. The company made the process of buying razors and grooming products easy and hassle-free, and their humorous marketing campaigns added a fun and relatable element to the brand.

The lesson to be learned from Dollar Shave Club's success is that a subscription-based business model and a focus on customer experience can lead to loyal customers and recurring revenue.

Airbnb:

Airbnb is an online marketplace that connects travelers with local hosts who offer short-term lodging. Founded in 2008, the company disrupted the traditional hospitality industry by offering travelers a more authentic and personalized travel experience.

What made Airbnb successful was its ability to create a trusted community of hosts and guests. The company implemented a thorough verification process for hosts and guests, and provided a secure platform for transactions and communication.

Airbnb's success also came from its focus on user experience. The company made the process of booking accommodations easy and convenient, and its search and recommendation algorithms helped guests find the perfect lodging for their needs.

The lesson to be learned from Airbnb's success is that creating a trusted community and a focus on user experience can lead to success in the sharing economy.

In conclusion, studying successful niche businesses can provide valuable insights into what it takes to build a successful business. From unique business models to a focus on social responsibility, subscription-based models to a focus on customer experience, and creating a trusted community to a focus on user experience, these case studies show that there are many paths to success in finding your niche. By learning from the successes and failures of others, you can increase your chances of building a successful niche business.

IX. Conclusion

In this chapter, we've covered the importance of finding a niche market in entrepreneurship and the steps involved in identifying, evaluating, and refining your niche business. To recap, let's review the key points covered in this chapter.

Firstly, we've defined niche markets and discussed the benefits of targeting a specific market segment. We've also examined successful niche businesses such as Dollar Shave Club, Warby Parker, and Airbnb, to name a few. These businesses have effectively identified a gap in the market and developed unique value propositions that resonate with their target audience.

Secondly, we've talked about assessing your skills and interests and finding overlap between them and market opportunities. We've discussed how to conduct market research, analyze market trends and consumer behavior, and identify your competitors and their strengths and weaknesses.

Thirdly, we've delved into creating your unique value proposition, defining your brand and positioning, and identifying your target audience.

Crafting a clear and compelling value proposition that differentiates you from your competitors is crucial to attracting and retaining customers in a crowded market. Fourthly, we've looked at launching a pilot test, gathering customer feedback, and refining your product or service offering. These steps are crucial to ensure that your business is meeting the needs of your target audience and to make any necessary adjustments before scaling your business.

Lastly, we've discussed strategies for growth and expansion, developing systems and processes, and building a strong team. Scaling your niche business requires careful planning and execution to maintain the unique value proposition that you've developed and to ensure that your business can grow sustainably.

In conclusion, finding your niche market is essential to entrepreneurship success. By identifying a gap in the market and developing a unique value proposition that resonates with your target audience, you can create a successful business that dominates the game and crushes the competition. Remember that finding your niche is not a one-time event, but an ongoing process of evaluation and refinement. Stay focused, stay hungry, and hustle harder to build the business of your dreams.

"Your time is limited, don't waste it living someone else's life"

- Steve Jobs

Chapter 3: Building Your Brand

I. **Introduction**
- Importance of building a strong brand in entrepreneurship
- Overview of the chapter

II. **Defining Your Brand Identity**
- Identifying your brand's values and personality
- Developing a brand mission statement
- Creating a brand style guide

III. **Brand Messaging**
- Crafting a compelling brand story
- Developing a brand voice and tone
- Creating a messaging framework

IV. **Brand Visuals**
- Designing a logo and visual identity
- Developing brand guidelines for typography, color, and imagery
- Creating a consistent brand aesthetic across all touchpoints

V. **Building Your Online Presence**
- Developing a website that reflects your brand
- Leveraging social media to build your brand
- Optimizing your online presence for search engines

VI. **Building Your Offline Presence**
- Developing a physical presence that reflects your brand
- Leveraging events and experiences to build your brand
- Using packaging and collateral to reinforce your brand

VII. Brand Management
- Managing brand reputation and crisis communications
- Developing a plan for ongoing brand evolution and growth
- Ensuring consistency across all brand touchpoints

VIII. Case Studies of Successful Niche Businesses
- Analysis of successful brands and their strategies
- Lessons learned from their experiences

IX. Conclusion
- Recap of key points
- Encouragement to prioritize brand building in entrepreneurship.

Chapter 3: Building Your Brand

I. **Introduction**

Building a strong brand is an essential component of any successful business venture, and it is especially crucial for entrepreneurs who are trying to carve out a niche for themselves in a competitive market. A brand represents the identity of a business and is a reflection of its values, mission, and personality. A strong brand can help entrepreneurs establish credibility, build customer loyalty, and differentiate themselves from their competitors.

In today's highly connected and digital world, creating a strong brand has become more critical than ever. With the rise of social media and other digital platforms, businesses can reach a wider audience and connect with customers more easily than ever before. However, this also means that competition is fierce, and businesses need to work hard to stand out in a crowded marketplace.

Building a strong brand requires a clear understanding of your business's identity and its target audience. You need to know what sets you apart from your competitors and what value you can provide to your customers. You also need to develop a brand strategy that aligns with your business goals and values.

One of the essential aspects of building a strong brand is consistency. Your brand should be consistent across all channels, from your website to your social media profiles and your marketing materials. Consistency helps build brand recognition and creates a sense of trust and reliability among your customers.

Overall, building a strong brand is an ongoing process that requires effort and commitment. It takes time to establish a brand identity and build a loyal customer base, but the benefits are well worth it. In this chapter, we will explore the different aspects of building a brand, including developing a brand strategy, creating a brand identity, and leveraging digital channels to build brand awareness.

II. Defining Your Brand Identity

When building a brand, it's important to have a clear understanding of your brand's values and personality. This will help you create a brand that is both authentic and appealing to your target audience. In this section, we'll discuss how to identify your brand's values and personality, develop a brand mission statement, and create a brand style guide.

Identifying Your Brand's Values and Personality:

Your brand's values are the guiding principles that define your company's culture, operations, and interactions with customers. These values should be clear, concise, and aligned with your overall business strategy. To identify your brand's values, ask yourself the following questions:

- **What is important to us as a company?**
- **What do we stand for?**
- **What are our core beliefs?**
- **What makes us different from our competitors?**
- **How do we want to be perceived by our customers?**

Once you have identified your brand's values, it's important to communicate them clearly to your employees and customers. This will help to build trust and loyalty among your customer base.

In addition to values, your brand also has a personality. This is the set of human characteristics that are associated with your brand.

For example, **Apple** is often associated with *innovation* and *creativity*, while **Nike** is associated with *athleticism* and *empowerment*. To identify your brand's personality, ask yourself:

- **If our brand was a person, what kind of person would it be?**
- **How do we want our customers to feel when they interact with our brand?**
- **What kind of language and tone should we use in our marketing materials?**
- **What kind of visuals should we use to represent our brand?**

Developing a Brand Mission Statement:

Your brand mission statement is a brief statement that summarizes your company's purpose and values. It should be clear, concise, and memorable. A well-crafted mission statement can help to guide your company's decision-making and inspire your employees to work towards a common goal. To develop your brand mission statement, ask yourself the following questions:

- **What is our company's purpose?**
- **What value do we bring to our customers?**
- **How do we want to impact the world?**

Use the answers to these questions to craft a mission statement that accurately reflects your brand's values and purpose.

Creating a Brand Style Guide:

A brand style guide is a document that outlines the visual and language guidelines for your brand. It includes information on things like logo usage, color palettes, typography, and tone of voice. A well-designed brand style guide can help to ensure consistency across all of your marketing materials and make it easier for your team to create new content.

When creating a brand style guide, be sure to include the following elements:

- **Logo usage guidelines**
- **Color palettes**
- **Typography guidelines**
- **Photography and illustration guidelines**
- **Tone of voice guidelines**

Your brand style guide should be accessible to all members of your team and updated regularly to reflect any changes to your brand's visual or language identity.

Conclusion

Defining your brand identity is an essential step in building a strong brand. By identifying your brand's values and personality, developing a mission statement, and creating a brand style guide, you can create a brand that is authentic, appealing, and consistent across all marketing materials. Remember, your brand is more than just a logo or a name – it's the sum total of all the interactions that customers have with your company. By putting in the time and effort to develop a strong brand identity, you can build a loyal customer base and stand out from the competition.

III. Brand Messaging

Effective brand messaging is crucial for building a strong brand and connecting with your target audience. Your brand messaging should convey your brand story, values, personality, and positioning in a way that resonates with your audience and differentiates you from competitors. In this section, we'll explore the key elements of brand messaging and how to create a messaging framework that guides your communication strategy.

Crafting a compelling brand story:

A brand story is a narrative that explains who you are, what you stand for, and why you exist.

It's an opportunity to humanize your brand and create an emotional connection with your audience. A good brand story should be authentic, memorable, and aligned with your brand values and mission.

To craft your brand story, start by defining your brand's unique selling proposition (USP) and the pain points your product or service solves for your target customers. Use storytelling techniques such as anecdotes, metaphors, or visual elements to make your story more engaging and relatable. You can also involve your customers in your brand story by featuring their experiences and testimonials.

Developing a brand voice and tone

Your brand voice and tone are the personality and style that you use to communicate with your audience. They should be consistent across all your brand touchpoints, from social media posts to customer service interactions. Your brand voice and tone should reflect your brand values, audience, and desired perception.

To develop your brand voice, consider the following:

- **Who is your target audience?**
- **What emotions do you want to evoke?**
- **What are your brand values?**
- **What is your brand personality?**
- **What kind of language and tone are appropriate for your industry?**

Your brand tone can vary depending on the context and channel, but it should still be consistent with your brand voice. For example, your tone can be more conversational on social media and more formal in a white paper.

Creating a messaging framework

A messaging framework is a tool that outlines the key messages you want to communicate to your target audience. It provides a structure for your brand messaging and ensures consistency across all your communication channels. A messaging framework should include the following:

- Value proposition: a clear and concise statement of the benefit your product or service offers to your customers
- Brand positioning: how you want your brand to be perceived in relation to competitors
- Key messages: the main points you want to convey to your audience, including your brand story, benefits, and features
- Proof points: evidence that supports your claims, such as statistics, testimonials, or awards
- Call to action: a clear and compelling request for your audience to take action, such as signing up for a trial or buying your product

By creating a messaging framework, you can ensure that all your communication aligns with your brand values and objectives and that you deliver a consistent message across all channels.

Conclusion

Crafting compelling brand messaging is a fundamental aspect of building a strong brand. By creating a brand story, developing a brand voice and tone, and creating a messaging framework, you can ensure that your brand messaging resonates with your target audience, communicates your unique value proposition, and differentiates you from competitors.

IV. Brand Visuals

When it comes to building a brand, visual identity is one of the most important components. Your brand visuals are the visual representation of your brand, and they should be instantly recognizable and memorable. Your brand visuals should not only look great but should also communicate the values and personality of your brand.

Designing a logo and visual identity A logo is the cornerstone of any brand's visual identity. It's the first thing people think of when they hear your brand's name and the visual that represents your brand. When designing a logo, you should consider the values and personality of your brand. Your logo should be unique, timeless, and memorable. It should also be versatile and work across different mediums, such as print and digital.

Once you have your logo, you can then start developing your brand's visual identity. Your visual identity should include typography, color, and imagery guidelines. Typography refers to the fonts used in your branding materials. You should choose a font that is easy to read and reflects the personality of your brand. Color is also an essential aspect of your visual identity, as it can evoke emotions and feelings. You should choose a color palette that is consistent with your brand's personality and values. Imagery is also important, as it can help communicate the personality of your brand. You should choose imagery that reflects your brand's values and personality.

Developing brand guidelines for typography, color, and imagery: Brand guidelines are a set of rules that dictate how your brand should be represented visually. They ensure consistency and help maintain the integrity of your brand. Your brand guidelines should include guidelines for typography, color, and imagery. Typography guidelines should specify which fonts to use for headlines, body text, and other design elements. Color guidelines should specify the colors to use for your brand, including primary and secondary colors. Imagery guidelines should specify the types of imagery to use and how to use them.

Creating a consistent brand aesthetic across all touchpoints: Consistency is key when it comes to branding. Your brand visuals should be consistent across all touchpoints, including your website, social media, packaging, and marketing materials. This consistency helps create a cohesive brand image and makes your brand more memorable. When designing your branding materials, you should keep your brand guidelines in mind and ensure that they are being followed consistently.

In conclusion, brand visuals are an essential component of building a strong brand. Your logo and visual identity should reflect the personality and values of your brand. Developing brand guidelines for typography, color, and imagery will ensure consistency across all touchpoints. Creating a consistent brand aesthetic will help make your brand more memorable and increase brand recognition. By investing time and effort into your brand visuals, you can build a strong brand that stands out from the competition.

V. Building Your Online Presence

In today's world, having a strong online presence is crucial for any business. As more and more consumers turn to the internet to research and make purchasing decisions, building a strong online presence has become a necessity. In this section, we will explore the steps you can take to build your online presence and increase your brand's visibility.

Developing a website that reflects your brand:

Your website is often the first point of contact for potential customers, and it is essential to make a good impression. Your website should reflect your brand identity and values, and be easy to navigate. Here are some tips for developing a website that reflects your brand:

- **Choose a design that matches your brand aesthetic:** The design of your website should align with your brand's visual identity. Use your brand colors, fonts, and imagery to create a cohesive look and feel.
- **Showcase your brand story:** Use your website to tell your brand's story and share your mission and values. This will help customers connect with your brand on a deeper level.
- **Make it easy to navigate:** Your website should be easy to navigate and find the information that customers are looking for. Use clear headings, menus, and calls-to-action to guide customers through your website.
- **Optimize for mobile:** More than half of all website traffic comes from mobile devices, so it is essential to ensure that your website is optimized for mobile devices. Use responsive design to ensure that your website looks great on any device.

Leveraging social media to build your brand: Social media is a powerful tool for building your brand and engaging with customers. With billions of people using social media every day, it is an excellent way to reach a large audience. Here are some tips for leveraging social media to build your brand:
- **Choose the right platforms:** There are many social media platforms available, and it is essential to choose the ones that are most relevant to your brand and target audience. For example, if you are targeting a younger audience, platforms like Instagram and TikTok may be more effective.
- **Create engaging content:** To build your brand on social media, you need to create content that is engaging and shareable. Use a mix of text, images, and videos to keep your audience interested.
- **Engage with your audience:** Social media is a two-way conversation, and it is essential to engage with your audience. Respond to comments and messages, and use social media to ask for feedback and opinions.
- **Consistency is key:** To build a strong brand on social media, it is essential to be consistent. Post regularly and at the same times each day to ensure that your audience knows when to expect new content.

Optimizing your online presence for search engines: Search engine optimization (SEO) is the process of optimizing your website and online presence to rank higher in search engine results pages (SERPs). By optimizing your online presence for search engines, you can increase your brand's visibility and attract more organic traffic. Here are some tips for optimizing your online presence for search engines:

- **Conduct keyword research:** Keyword research involves identifying the keywords and phrases that your target audience is searching for. Use tools like Google Keyword Planner to identify relevant keywords and phrases.
- **Optimize your website:** Use the keywords and phrases you identified in your keyword research to optimize your website. This includes optimizing your meta tags, headings, and content.
- **Build backlinks:** Backlinks are links from other websites to your website. They are a crucial factor in SEO and can help to increase your website's authority and visibility. Reach out to other websites in your industry and ask if they would be willing to link to your website.
- **Monitor your results:** SEO is an ongoing process, and it is essential to monitor your results to see what is working and what isn't. Use tools like Google Analytics to track.

VI. Building Your Offline Presence

In today's digital age, it's easy to overlook the importance of building an offline presence for your brand. While online channels such as websites and social media are essential for reaching a wider audience, building a physical presence is equally important for creating a memorable and impactful brand experience. In this section, we'll explore the different ways you can build your offline presence and create a tangible connection with your audience.

Developing a physical presence that reflects your brand: Your brand's physical presence should be a reflection of your brand's identity and values.

Whether you're opening a brick-and-mortar store or attending a trade show, your physical presence should convey your brand's story and mission. The space should be designed in a way that is consistent with your brand's visual identity and the overall customer experience should align with your brand values. For instance, if you're a luxury brand, your physical space should feel luxurious and high-end. If you're a brand focused on sustainability, your space should be eco-friendly and sustainable.

Leveraging events and experiences to build your brand: Attending events and hosting experiences are great ways to build your brand offline. Events and experiences provide an opportunity for your audience to interact with your brand in a tangible way, creating a more memorable and impactful brand experience. Consider attending trade shows, hosting pop-up shops, or organizing experiential events to showcase your products and services. These events not only help to build brand awareness but also create an emotional connection with your audience.

Using packaging and collateral to reinforce your brand: Your brand's packaging and collateral should be consistent with your brand identity and values. They are an extension of your brand's story and help to reinforce your brand message in a tangible way. Your packaging should be designed in a way that aligns with your brand's visual identity and your brand values. For example, if you're a brand that values sustainability, your packaging should be eco-friendly and made of recycled materials. If you're a luxury brand, your packaging should feel high-end and luxurious. Similarly, your collateral such as business cards, brochures, and other promotional materials should also align with your brand's identity and values.

In summary, building an offline presence for your brand is crucial for creating a memorable and impactful brand experience. Your physical presence, events and experiences, and packaging and collateral are all important elements that contribute to building a strong offline brand presence. By focusing on creating a consistent and aligned brand identity across all touchpoints, you can build a lasting connection with your audience both online and offline.

VII. **Brand Management**

In the modern world, where brands are becoming increasingly important for businesses of all sizes, effective brand management has become crucial for long-term success. In this section, we will discuss the importance of brand management, how to manage your brand effectively, and the key elements of a successful brand management strategy.

Why is Brand Management Important?

A brand is more than just a logo or a name. It encompasses everything that a business represents, including its values, personality, messaging, and visual identity. Effective brand management is essential to ensure that your brand is perceived the way you want it to be and that it remains relevant and consistent over time.

Brand management is especially important when it comes to reputation and crisis management. A negative review or customer experience can damage a brand's reputation and affect its bottom line. Effective brand management strategies can help mitigate these risks by proactively monitoring and addressing potential issues before they become major problems.

Key Elements of Brand Management:
1. **Brand Audits**: Conducting regular brand audits is a key component of effective brand management. A brand audit involves assessing how your brand is perceived by your customers and stakeholders, identifying areas of strength and weakness, and making necessary changes to improve brand perception.
2. **Brand Guidelines**: Brand guidelines are a set of rules and standards that define how your brand should be represented across all channels, including visual identity, messaging, and tone of voice. They serve as a guide for all stakeholders to ensure consistency and continuity in your brand's representation.
3. **Reputation Management**: Reputation management involves monitoring and addressing any negative comments or reviews about your brand. This includes having a crisis communication plan in place to address any issues that may arise quickly and effectively.
4. **Evolution and Growth**: Brands are not static, and they must evolve and grow to remain relevant. Effective brand management involves constantly reviewing and evolving your brand to reflect changing market trends and customer needs.
5. **Consistency**: Consistency is key when it comes to brand management. All brand touchpoints, including online and offline, must represent your brand consistently, ensuring that customers and stakeholders have a clear and consistent perception of your brand.

Effective brand management is a crucial aspect of building a successful and long-lasting brand. By conducting regular brand audits, creating clear brand guidelines, developing a reputation management strategy, constantly evolving and growing your brand, and ensuring consistency across all touchpoints, you can effectively manage your brand and maintain its relevance and consistency over time. In a world where brands are becoming increasingly important, strong brand management is essential for businesses of all sizes.

VIII. Case Studies of Successful Brand Building

One of the best ways to learn about building a successful brand is by studying the strategies and experiences of other successful brands. By analyzing their approach and lessons learned, you can gain valuable insights and apply them to your own brand-building efforts. In this chapter, we will explore some case studies of successful brand building and discuss the key takeaways.

1. **Nike**

Nike is a global athletic wear brand that has become synonymous with high-performance sports gear. Over the years, the company has built an iconic brand identity that appeals to athletes and fitness enthusiasts of all levels. Nike's brand-building success can be attributed to a few key factors:

- **Consistency**: Nike has maintained a consistent brand identity across all its products, marketing campaigns, and communications. From its iconic swoosh logo to its famous "Just Do It" slogan, Nike's brand messaging and visual identity have remained constant over the years.

- **Emotional Appeal**: Nike has managed to tap into the emotional aspect of sports and fitness, positioning itself as a brand that helps people achieve their goals and overcome challenges. Its marketing campaigns often feature inspiring stories of real-life athletes who have overcome obstacles and achieved success.
- **Innovation**: Nike has always been at the forefront of innovation, constantly pushing the boundaries of athletic wear technology to create products that deliver exceptional performance. This commitment to innovation has helped Nike stay ahead of the competition and maintain its leadership position in the market.

Key Takeaways:
- Consistency in brand messaging and visual identity is crucial for building a strong brand.
- Emotional appeal can be a powerful tool in building a brand that resonates with people.
- Innovation is essential for staying ahead of the competition and maintaining brand leadership.

2. **Apple**

Apple is a technology brand that has revolutionized the consumer electronics industry with its innovative products and design. Apple's brand-building success can be attributed to a few key factors:

- **Design**: Apple's products are known for their sleek, minimalist design, which has become a key part of its brand identity. This design philosophy has helped Apple stand out in a crowded market and appeal to consumers who value aesthetics.

- **User Experience**: Apple's products are designed to provide a seamless user experience, with intuitive interfaces and features that make them easy to use. This commitment to user experience has helped Apple build a loyal customer base that keeps coming back for more.
- **Brand Ecosystem**: Apple has created a brand ecosystem that includes not only its products but also its services, such as iTunes and the App Store. This ecosystem has helped Apple build a strong brand community that is invested in the brand and its products.

Key Takeaways:
- Design can be a powerful tool for creating a distinctive brand identity.
- User experience is essential for building a loyal customer base.
- Building a brand ecosystem can help create a strong brand community.

3. Coca-Cola

Coca-Cola is a global beverage brand that has become one of the most recognizable brands in the world. Coca-Cola's brand-building success can be attributed to a few key factors:

- **Emotional Connection**: Coca-Cola has built a brand that is all about happiness and sharing special moments with loved ones. Its marketing campaigns often feature heartwarming stories of people coming together and enjoying Coca-Cola.
- **Consistency**: Coca-Cola has maintained a consistent brand identity over the years, from its iconic red and white logo to its famous jingle. This consistency has helped Coca-Cola become one of the most recognized brands in the world.

- **Brand Extensions**: Coca-Cola has successfully extended its brand into different product categories, such as Diet Coke, Coca-Cola Zero, and Sprite. These brand extensions have helped Coca-Cola appeal to different segments of the market and expand its reach.

Key Takeaways:
- Emotional connection can be a powerful tool in building

IX. Conclusion

In this chapter, we have explored the various components of building a strong and effective brand. We have discussed the importance of having a clear brand message, a consistent visual identity, a strong online and offline presence, and a plan for ongoing brand management and evolution. We have also analyzed successful brands and the strategies they have used to build their brands.

As an entrepreneur, building your brand is one of the most important things you can do to ensure the success of your business. A strong brand not only helps you stand out from the competition, but it also creates a connection with your customers and builds trust and loyalty.

To recap some of the key points we have discussed:
- Crafting a compelling brand story is essential in creating an emotional connection with your customers.
- Developing a brand voice and tone that reflects your brand personality and values is important in creating a consistent and authentic brand identity.
- Creating a messaging framework that defines your brand positioning, key messages, and target audience helps guide your brand communication.

- Designing a logo and visual identity, developing brand guidelines for typography, color, and imagery, and creating a consistent brand aesthetic across all touchpoints help create a strong and recognizable brand.
- Building an online presence through a website and social media, and optimizing for search engines is crucial in reaching and engaging with your target audience.
- Building an offline presence through physical locations, events, and packaging and collateral helps reinforce your brand and create memorable experiences for your customers.
- Managing your brand reputation and having a plan for ongoing brand evolution and growth is important in ensuring the longevity and success of your brand.
- Learning from successful brand case studies can provide valuable insights and inspiration for building your own brand.
- In conclusion, building a strong and effective brand is a continuous process that requires time, effort, and attention. As an entrepreneur, prioritizing your brand-building efforts can help differentiate your business and create a lasting impact on your customers. So, hustle harder and build a brand that dominates the game and crushes your competition.

"A brand for a company is like a reputation for a person. You earn a reputation by trying to do hard things well."

- Jeff Bezos

Chapter 4: Developing a Winning Strategy

I. **Introduction**
- Importance of having a winning strategy
- Overview of the chapter

II. **Understanding the Market and Your Competitors**
- Conducting market research
- Analyzing the competition
- Identifying customer needs and pain points

III. **Defining Your Unique Value Proposition**
- Understanding what makes your brand unique
- Crafting a compelling value proposition
- Communicating your value proposition effectively

IV. **Setting Goals and Objectives**
- Defining long-term and short-term goals
- Identifying key performance indicators (KPIs)
- Developing action plans to achieve goals

V. **Crafting Your Business Model**
- Choosing a business model that aligns with your goals
- Identifying revenue streams
- Developing pricing strategies

VI. **Developing a Marketing and Sales Plan**
- Identifying target audiences and personas
- Developing a marketing and sales funnel
- Creating a promotional mix that aligns with your goals

VII. Building Your Team and Infrastructure
- Identifying key roles and responsibilities
- Developing systems and processes
- Creating a culture that aligns with your values

VIII. Execution and Measurement
- Implementing your strategy
- Monitoring and measuring progress
- Adjusting your strategy as needed

IX. Case Studies of Successful Strategies
- Analysis of successful brands and their strategies
- Lessons learned from their experiences

X. Conclusion
- Recap of key points
- Encouragement to develop and execute a winning strategy

Chapter 4: Developing a Winning Strategy

Chapter 4 of "Hustle Harder: How to Dominate the Game and Crush Your Competition" is all about developing a winning strategy. This is a crucial aspect of entrepreneurship, as having a well thought-out strategy can mean the difference between success and failure in the business world.

In the first section of this chapter, we'll explore the importance of having a winning strategy and provide an overview of what readers can expect to learn from this chapter.

Having a winning strategy is critical because it helps you achieve your goals and stay focused on what matters most. Whether you're starting a new business or growing an existing one, having a clear strategy in place will guide your decision-making, enable you to prioritize tasks, and provide a roadmap to success.

The first step to developing a winning strategy is to understand your business's unique strengths and weaknesses. This involves conducting a SWOT analysis to identify your company's strengths, weaknesses, opportunities, and threats. By doing so, you can better understand where you stand in the market and what you need to do to succeed.

Another important aspect of developing a winning strategy is to have a clear understanding of your target market. Who are your customers? What do they need and want? What are their pain points? By understanding your customers' needs and wants, you can tailor your products and services to meet their needs, which will increase your chances of success.

In this chapter, we'll also explore how to set SMART goals - specific, measurable, achievable, relevant, and time-bound - to help you achieve your objectives. We'll cover the different types of goals you should set, how to prioritize them, and how to track your progress towards achieving them.

Finally, we'll discuss the importance of being flexible and adaptable in your strategy. No strategy is perfect, and as you grow and evolve, your strategy may need to change as well. By being open to change and willing to adapt, you can stay ahead of the competition and continue to grow your business.

Overall, this chapter will provide readers with a comprehensive understanding of what it takes to develop a winning strategy. We'll cover the essential components of a successful strategy, provide practical tips and tools for developing one, and explore case studies of successful entrepreneurs who have developed winning strategies of their own.

In the business world, understanding the market and your competitors is essential to developing a winning strategy. Conducting market research, analyzing the competition, and identifying customer needs and pain points are the key steps in this process.

Market research is the process of collecting and analyzing information about a market, including customer behavior, market size, and trends. This information can help entrepreneurs identify opportunities, assess the feasibility of their business ideas, and make informed decisions about their products or services.

To conduct market research, entrepreneurs can use various methods such as surveys, focus groups, and data analysis tools. These methods can provide valuable insights into customer behavior, preferences, and attitudes towards a particular product or service.

Analyzing the competition is another critical aspect of understanding the market. This involves identifying and assessing the strengths and weaknesses of competitors, their products or services, pricing strategies, marketing efforts, and customer base. This information can help entrepreneurs identify opportunities to differentiate their products or services and develop a competitive advantage.

Entrepreneurs can use various methods to analyze the competition, such as SWOT analysis, Porter's Five Forces analysis, and market share analysis. These methods can help entrepreneurs understand the competitive landscape and identify opportunities to outperform their competitors.

Identifying customer needs and pain points is also crucial in developing a winning strategy. Entrepreneurs must understand their target customers' needs and problems to develop products or services that solve their problems and meet their needs.

To identify customer needs and pain points, entrepreneurs can use methods such as customer surveys, focus groups, and social media analysis. These methods can provide valuable insights into customer behavior, preferences, and attitudes towards a particular product or service.

In conclusion, understanding the market and your competitors is a critical step in developing a winning strategy. Conducting market research, analyzing the competition, and identifying customer needs and pain points can provide valuable insights that entrepreneurs can use to differentiate their products or services, develop a competitive advantage, and meet their customers' needs.

Developing a unique value proposition is an essential step in developing a winning strategy for your business.

Your value proposition defines what sets you apart from your competitors, and it communicates the value you provide to your customers. In this section, we'll explore how to craft a compelling value proposition and communicate it effectively to your target audience.

Understanding What Makes Your Brand Unique: To develop a unique value proposition, you first need to understand what makes your brand stand out from the competition. This involves identifying your unique selling points, such as the features and benefits of your products or services that your competitors can't match. You should also consider your brand's personality, voice, and mission, and how these elements contribute to your unique identity.

Crafting a Compelling Value Proposition: Once you have a clear understanding of what makes your brand unique, you can begin crafting a compelling value proposition. Your value proposition should clearly communicate the benefits of your products or services to your target audience, highlighting how they solve a particular problem or meet a specific need.

A good value proposition should be:

- **Clear and concise**: Your value proposition should be easy to understand and communicate the most important benefits of your products or services in a few simple sentences.
- **Unique**: Your value proposition should emphasize what sets your brand apart from the competition, highlighting the features and benefits that your competitors can't match.
- **Customer-focused**: Your value proposition should focus on the benefits that your customers will receive, rather than simply listing the features of your products or services.

- **Memorable**: Your value proposition should be memorable and catchy, making it easy for your target audience to remember and recall.

Communicating Your Value Proposition Effectively: Once you've crafted a compelling value proposition, it's essential to communicate it effectively to your target audience. This involves incorporating your value proposition into your brand messaging across all channels, including your website, social media profiles, marketing materials, and sales pitches.

To communicate your value proposition effectively, you should:

- **Use clear and concise language**: Use language that is easy to understand and avoids jargon or technical terms that your target audience may not be familiar with.
- **Highlight the benefits**: Emphasize the benefits of your products or services, and how they solve a particular problem or meet a specific need.
- **Use visual elements**: Incorporate visual elements into your brand messaging, such as images and videos, to help communicate your value proposition more effectively.
- **Be consistent**: Ensure that your value proposition is consistent across all channels so that your target audience receives a consistent message about your brand.

In conclusion, developing a unique value proposition and communicating it effectively to your target audience is critical to developing a winning strategy for your business. By understanding what makes your brand unique, crafting a compelling value proposition, and communicating it effectively across all channels, you can differentiate your brand from the competition and win the loyalty of your target audience.

Setting clear and achievable goals and objectives is essential for any business to succeed. It is important to define both long-term and short-term goals as well as identifying key performance indicators (KPIs) that will measure progress towards those goals. Once these are defined, a solid action plan can be developed to achieve them.

Defining Long-Term and Short-Term Goals

Long-term goals provide a clear vision of where the business wants to be in the future. They typically span multiple years and are often used as a guiding principle for decision making. Short-term goals, on the other hand, are more immediate and focus on achieving specific outcomes within a shorter period of time, such as a few months or a year.

When defining goals, it is important to make them specific, measurable, achievable, relevant, and time-bound (SMART). Specific goals are clear and well-defined, while measurable goals can be quantified and tracked. Achievable goals should be realistic and within reach, relevant goals align with the business's overall strategy, and time-bound goals have a specific deadline.

Identifying Key Performance Indicators (KPIs):

KPIs are metrics used to track progress towards goals and objectives. They provide a clear understanding of how well the business is performing and whether it is on track to achieve its goals. KPIs can be financial, such as revenue growth or profit margins, or non-financial, such as customer satisfaction or employee retention rates.

When identifying KPIs, it is important to focus on those that are most relevant to the business's goals and objectives. Too many KPIs can be overwhelming and lead to a lack of focus, while too few can result in a lack of insight into key areas of the business

Developing Action Plans:
Once goals and KPIs are defined, a solid action plan can be developed to achieve them. This plan should include specific tasks, timelines, and responsibilities for achieving each goal. It should also outline any necessary resources and potential obstacles that may need to be overcome.

Regular monitoring and tracking of progress towards goals and KPIs is essential to ensure that the action plan is effective and on track. If progress is not being made, adjustments may need to be made to the plan or new strategies may need to be implemented.

Conclusion

Setting goals and objectives is an essential part of developing a winning strategy. By defining clear and achievable goals, identifying relevant KPIs, and developing a solid action plan, businesses can achieve success and growth. Regular monitoring and adjustments can help ensure that the business stays on track towards achieving its goals and objectives.

In order to develop a winning strategy, it is important to carefully craft your business model. A business model is a framework that outlines how a company creates, delivers, and captures value. Choosing the right business model can be the difference between success and failure in a highly competitive market. In this section, we will explore some key considerations for crafting your business model.

Choosing a business model that aligns with your goals:
Your business model should be designed to achieve your long-term goals.

There are many different business models to choose from, including:
- **Direct sales**: You sell your products or services directly to customers.
- **Subscription**: Customers pay a recurring fee to access your products or services.
- **Freemium**: You offer a basic version of your product or service for free, and charge for premium features.
- **Marketplace**: You provide a platform for buyers and sellers to transact, and take a commission on each sale.
- **Licensing**: You sell the rights to use your intellectual property to other companies.

It is important to choose a business model that aligns with your goals and the needs of your target market. For example, if your goal is to generate recurring revenue, a subscription model may be the best option. If you have a unique product or service that can be licensed, this may be a better fit for your business.

Identifying revenue streams:

Once you have chosen your business model, it is important to identify your revenue streams. This includes understanding how you will generate revenue from each customer or transaction. For example, if you are using a subscription model, your revenue stream will be based on the recurring fees you charge your customers. If you are using a marketplace model, your revenue stream will be based on the commission you charge on each transaction.

It is important to carefully consider your revenue streams and ensure that they are sustainable over the long term. This may involve testing different pricing strategies, offering different levels of service, or exploring new revenue streams.

Developing pricing strategies

Pricing is a critical component of any business model.

You need to ensure that your pricing strategy is competitive, while also allowing you to generate a profit. There are many different pricing strategies to consider, including:

- **Cost-plus pricing**: You add a markup to your costs to determine your selling price.
- **Value-based pricing**: You set your prices based on the value that your product or service provides to customers.
- **Dynamic pricing**: You adjust your prices in real-time based on market demand, competition, or other factors.

It is important to carefully consider your pricing strategy and test different approaches to determine what works best for your business.

In conclusion, crafting your business model is a critical component of developing a winning strategy. You need to choose a business model that aligns with your long-term goals, identify sustainable revenue streams, and develop a pricing strategy that allows you to generate a profit while remaining competitive. By taking these steps, you can ensure that your business model is designed to succeed in a highly competitive market.

In today's highly competitive business landscape, developing a marketing and sales plan is essential to the success of any company. Without a clear plan in place, it is nearly impossible to attract and retain customers, generate leads, and ultimately drive revenue. In this section, we'll explore the key components of a successful marketing and sales plan, including identifying target audiences and personas, developing a marketing and sales funnel, and creating a promotional mix that aligns with your goals.

Identifying target audiences and personas:
The first step in developing a marketing and sales plan is to identify your target audiences and personas. This involves researching and analyzing your market to determine who your ideal customers are and what their needs and pain points are. By understanding your target audiences and personas, you can tailor your marketing and sales efforts to effectively reach and engage them.

One useful tool for identifying target audiences and personas is the creation of buyer personas. A buyer persona is a detailed profile of a specific type of customer that includes information such as their demographics, interests, challenges, and purchasing behavior. By creating detailed buyer personas, you can better understand your customers and create marketing and sales strategies that resonate with them.

Developing a marketing and sales funnel:
Once you've identified your target audiences and personas, the next step is to develop a marketing and sales funnel. A marketing and sales funnel is a visual representation of the steps that a customer takes from initial awareness of your brand to making a purchase. The funnel typically includes four stages: awareness, interest, decision, and action.

In the awareness stage, the goal is to create brand awareness and capture the attention of potential customers. This can be achieved through various marketing channels, such as social media, email marketing, and content marketing.

In the interest stage, the goal is to engage potential customers and educate them about your products or services. This can be done through various marketing tactics, such as webinars, case studies, and free trials.

In the decision stage, the goal is to convince potential customers to make a purchase.

This can be achieved through targeted advertising, customer reviews, and other persuasive tactics.

In the action stage, the goal is to convert potential customers into paying customers. This can be done through a variety of sales strategies, such as offering discounts, providing exceptional customer service, and streamlining the purchase process.

Creating a promotional mix that aligns with your goals:

Finally, in order to successfully execute your marketing and sales plan, it is essential to create a promotional mix that aligns with your goals. The promotional mix refers to the various marketing tactics that you will use to promote your brand and drive sales. This can include a mix of online and offline tactics, such as social media advertising, email marketing, direct mail, and events.

When creating your promotional mix, it is important to consider factors such as your budget, target audiences, and overall marketing goals. For example, if your target audience is primarily millennials, social media advertising may be a more effective tactic than traditional print advertising. Similarly, if your goal is to generate leads, a combination of email marketing and targeted advertising may be more effective than solely relying on social media.

In conclusion, developing a marketing and sales plan is a critical component of any winning strategy. By identifying your target audiences and personas, developing a marketing and sales funnel, and creating a promotional mix that aligns with your goals, you can effectively reach and engage your customers, generate leads, and ultimately drive revenue.

A successful business is not just about having a great idea or a well-defined strategy. It also requires a strong team and infrastructure to support it.

In this section, we will discuss the importance of building a team and infrastructure that aligns with your goals and values.

Identifying Key Roles and Responsibilities:

One of the first steps in building your team is identifying the key roles and responsibilities that are needed to achieve your goals. Depending on the size and nature of your business, these roles could include sales, marketing, operations, finance, and customer support, among others. It is important to identify these roles early on and to ensure that you have the right people in each position.

When hiring for these roles, look for individuals who not only have the necessary skills and experience but also share your vision and values. Consider conducting behavioral interviews that assess a candidate's personality, work ethic, and communication skills to ensure that they will be a good fit for your team.

Developing Systems and Processes:

To ensure that your business runs smoothly and efficiently, it is important to develop systems and processes for each area of your business. This includes everything from onboarding new employees to managing inventory to customer service.

By creating clear and well-defined systems and processes, you can ensure that everyone on your team knows what is expected of them and how to perform their job effectively. This can help to reduce errors, increase productivity, and improve overall performance.

Creating a Culture that Aligns with Your Values:

In addition to having the right team and infrastructure, it is important to create a culture that aligns with your values. This can help to foster a sense of community and shared purpose among your team members, which can lead to increased motivation, engagement, and productivity.

To create a strong culture, start by defining your values and communicating them clearly to your team. Encourage open and honest communication, and reward behaviors that align with your values. Consider hosting team-building activities and social events that can help to build camaraderie and strengthen your team's relationships.

Conclusion

Building a strong team and infrastructure is essential for any business looking to succeed in today's competitive marketplace. By identifying key roles and responsibilities, developing systems and processes, and creating a culture that aligns with your values, you can create a foundation for long-term success. Remember, your team is the backbone of your business, so invest in them wisely and watch your business thrive.

Once you have defined your winning strategy, it's time to put it into action. Execution is the key to success, and it requires a combination of focus, discipline, and flexibility. In this section, we will discuss how to implement your strategy, monitor and measure progress, and adjust your strategy as needed.

Implementing Your Strategy

Implementing your strategy requires discipline and focus. You need to break down your strategy into specific goals, and then create action plans to achieve those goals. This requires a clear understanding of your resources, timelines, and budgets.

It's important to assign specific responsibilities for each action item and to establish clear deadlines for completion. You should also establish systems and processes to ensure that everyone is on the same page and that progress is being made.

To ensure successful implementation, you need to communicate your strategy clearly and consistently to your team. Everyone needs to understand the goals, the action plans, and their specific responsibilities.

You should also establish regular check-ins to ensure that progress is being made and to identify any issues that need to be addressed.

Monitoring and Measuring Progress:

Once your strategy is being implemented, you need to monitor and measure progress. This involves tracking your key performance indicators (KPIs) and comparing them to your goals. KPIs are specific metrics that help you measure progress and identify areas for improvement.

KPIs can be related to revenue, customer acquisition, customer retention, product quality, or any other metric that is important to your business. The key is to identify the metrics that matter most and to track them consistently.

It's important to establish a regular cadence for reviewing your KPIs. This could be weekly, monthly, or quarterly depending on your business and your goals. You should also establish a process for reporting progress to your team and your stakeholders.

Adjusting Your Strategy as Needed:

As you monitor progress, you may find that you need to adjust your strategy. This could be due to changes in the market, unexpected challenges, or new opportunities. It's important to remain flexible and to be willing to adjust your strategy as needed.

When making adjustments, it's important to go back to your goals and your value proposition. You need to ensure that any changes you make are aligned with your overall strategy and your core values.

It's also important to communicate any changes to your team and stakeholders. Everyone needs to understand the new direction and how it impacts their responsibilities.

In conclusion, executing a winning strategy requires discipline, focus, and flexibility.

You should also establish regular check-ins to ensure that progress is being made and to identify any issues that need to be addressed.

Monitoring and Measuring Progress:

Once your strategy is being implemented, you need to monitor and measure progress. This involves tracking your key performance indicators (KPIs) and comparing them to your goals. KPIs are specific metrics that help you measure progress and identify areas for improvement.

KPIs can be related to revenue, customer acquisition, customer retention, product quality, or any other metric that is important to your business. The key is to identify the metrics that matter most and to track them consistently.

It's important to establish a regular cadence for reviewing your KPIs. This could be weekly, monthly, or quarterly depending on your business and your goals. You should also establish a process for reporting progress to your team and your stakeholders.

Adjusting Your Strategy as Needed:

As you monitor progress, you may find that you need to adjust your strategy. This could be due to changes in the market, unexpected challenges, or new opportunities. It's important to remain flexible and to be willing to adjust your strategy as needed.

When making adjustments, it's important to go back to your goals and your value proposition. You need to ensure that any changes you make are aligned with your overall strategy and your core values.

It's also important to communicate any changes to your team and stakeholders. Everyone needs to understand the new direction and how it impacts their responsibilities.

In conclusion, executing a winning strategy requires discipline, focus, and flexibility.

You need to break down your strategy into specific goals and action plans, communicate clearly with your team, monitor progress, and adjust your strategy as needed. By following these steps, you can achieve your goals and dominate the game. This section will analyze successful brands and their strategies and highlight the lessons learned from their experiences.

Case studies are a valuable tool for business owners and entrepreneurs looking to develop a winning strategy. By examining successful companies and their strategies, entrepreneurs can gain valuable insights into what works and what doesn't when it comes to growing a business. Some of the most successful brands in the world have implemented strategies that are both innovative and effective.

One such example is Apple, a company that has consistently been at the forefront of innovation and technology. Apple's success can be attributed to a number of factors, including their ability to create products that are both stylish and user-friendly. Their marketing campaigns are also a key factor in their success, as they have been able to create a loyal customer base through their innovative advertising campaigns.

Another example is Nike, a brand that has successfully positioned itself as a leader in the athletic apparel industry. Nike's success can be attributed to their ability to create high-quality products that appeal to athletes of all levels. Their marketing campaigns have also been a key factor in their success, as they have been able to create a strong emotional connection with their customers.

In addition to Apple and Nike, there are numerous other companies that have successfully implemented winning strategies. These companies include Amazon, Google, and Facebook, among others.

By examining these companies and their strategies, entrepreneurs can gain valuable insights into what it takes to create a successful business.

One of the key lessons that can be learned from successful case studies is the importance of innovation. In order to succeed in today's competitive marketplace, businesses must be willing to take risks and think outside the box. This means developing new products and services, as well as exploring new marketing strategies and channels.

Another important lesson is the importance of branding. Successful companies have strong and recognizable brands that resonate with their target audience. This means investing in branding efforts, such as logo design, website development, and advertising campaigns.

Finally, successful case studies highlight the importance of adaptability. The business landscape is constantly evolving, and companies must be able to adapt to changing market conditions in order to succeed. This means being flexible and willing to make changes to the business model as needed.

In conclusion, case studies of successful strategies provide valuable insights for entrepreneurs looking to develop a winning strategy. By examining the strategies of successful companies like Apple, Nike, and Amazon, entrepreneurs can learn important lessons about innovation, branding, and adaptability. With these insights in mind, entrepreneurs can develop strategies that are both innovative and effective, setting themselves up for success in today's competitive marketplace.

Chapter 4 of "Hustle Harder: How to Dominate the Game and Crush Your Competition" has provided an extensive guide to developing a winning strategy for your business.

It has covered a range of topics, including market research, defining your unique value proposition, setting goals and objectives, crafting your business model, developing a marketing and sales plan, building your team and infrastructure, execution and measurement, case studies of successful strategies, and a conclusion.

Now, as we reach the end of this chapter, it's essential to recap the key points and encourage readers to develop and execute a winning strategy.

Firstly, the importance of having a winning strategy cannot be overstated. In today's competitive business landscape, it's not enough to have a great product or service; you need a solid strategy that will set you apart from your competitors and drive your success. A winning strategy involves defining your unique value proposition, setting clear goals and objectives, identifying your target audience, developing a marketing and sales plan, building a strong team, and implementing and measuring your strategy.

Secondly, throughout this chapter, we have emphasized the importance of market research, understanding your competitors, and identifying customer needs and pain points. By conducting thorough research, you can gain a better understanding of the market and develop a strategy that is tailored to your target audience's needs and preferences. Analyzing your competitors can help you identify gaps in the market and develop a strategy that sets you apart. Additionally, identifying customer needs and pain points can help you create a product or service that addresses those needs and positions you as a solution provider.

Thirdly, we have discussed the importance of defining your unique value proposition and developing a pricing strategy that aligns with your goals.

Your value proposition should clearly communicate what sets you apart from your competitors and why customers should choose your product or service. Your pricing strategy should reflect your value proposition and the level of quality and service that you provide.

Fourthly, setting clear goals and objectives is essential to achieving success. By defining both long-term and short-term goals, you can create a roadmap for achieving your vision. Additionally, identifying key performance indicators (KPIs) can help you measure progress and adjust your strategy as needed.

Fifthly, crafting a business model that aligns with your goals is crucial. Your business model should reflect your unique value proposition and the revenue streams that will drive your success. Additionally, developing a marketing and sales plan that aligns with your goals can help you reach your target audience and drive sales.

Sixthly, building a strong team and infrastructure is essential to executing your strategy successfully. Identifying key roles and responsibilities, developing systems and processes, and creating a culture that aligns with your values can help you build a team that is committed to achieving your vision.

Seventhly, execution and measurement are critical to achieving success. Implementing your strategy, monitoring progress, and adjusting your approach as needed can help you stay on track and achieve your goals.

Lastly, we have discussed case studies of successful strategies and lessons learned from their experiences. By analyzing successful brands, we can gain valuable insights into what makes a winning strategy and how we can apply those lessons to our own businesses.

In conclusion, developing a winning strategy is essential to achieving success in today's competitive business landscape. By following the steps outlined in this chapter, you can create a strategy that sets you apart from your competitors and drives your success. Remember to conduct thorough market research, define your unique value proposition, set clear goals and objectives, develop a business model and marketing plan, build a strong team and infrastructure, and execute and measure your strategy.

"Strategy without tactics is the slowest route to victory. Tactics without strategy is the noise before defeat."

- Sun Tzu

Chapter 5: Hustling for Funding

I. **Introduction**
- Explanation of the importance of funding in business
- Overview of the chapter contents

II. **Types of Funding**
- Description of the different types of funding available to entrepreneurs
- Pros and cons of each type of funding

III. **Preparing for Funding**
- Understanding the requirements for obtaining funding
- Developing a strong business plan and pitch deck
- Building a strong network and relationships with potential investors

IV. **Finding the Right Investors**
- Identifying the right investors for your business
- Building relationships with investors
- Pitching your business to potential investors

V. **Negotiating and Closing the Deal**
- Understanding the negotiation process
- Tips for negotiating with investors
- Preparing for due diligence
- Closing the deal

VI. **Alternative Funding Sources**
- Overview of alternative funding sources
- Crowdfunding
- Grants
- Loans

VII. Case Studies
- Analysis of successful funding strategies
- Lessons learned from successful and unsuccessful funding attempts

VIII. Conclusion
- Recap of key points
- Encouragement to hustle for funding
- Final thoughts

Chapter 5: Hustling for Funding

I. **Introduction**

In the world of business, money talks. Funding is a critical aspect of any business venture, and without it, your dreams and aspirations might never come to fruition. This is especially true for startups and early-stage companies, which often require significant financial resources to develop and grow.

The importance of funding cannot be overstated. From covering startup costs to expanding your business, funding is what keeps the wheels turning. Without it, your business is likely to flounder, and your dreams may never be realized.

In this chapter, we will delve into the world of funding, exploring the various options available to entrepreneurs and business owners. We will look at the pros and cons of each option, helping you make an informed decision about which path to take.

We'll start by examining the different types of funding available and the criteria that investors use to evaluate potential investments. We will also discuss the importance of having a solid business plan and pitch deck when seeking funding, as well as strategies for networking and building relationships with potential investors.

Whether you're seeking venture capital, angel investment, crowdfunding, or other forms of funding, this chapter will provide you with the insights and tools you need to navigate the funding landscape with confidence.

So let's dive in and explore the exciting and often challenging world of funding.

By the end of this chapter, you'll have a solid understanding of the funding options available to you and how to position yourself for success in securing the funding your business needs to thrive.

II. **Types of Funding**

When it comes to starting a business or taking an existing business to the next level, one of the biggest challenges entrepreneurs face is securing funding. While many entrepreneurs have a great idea and a solid business plan, without the financial resources to back it up, their plans may never come to fruition.

In this chapter, we will explore the different types of funding available to entrepreneurs and the pros and cons of each. This information can help you make informed decisions when it comes to financing your business.

Bootstrapping:

Bootstrapping is the process of starting or growing a business using personal savings, revenue from sales, or operating cash flow. In other words, you fund your own business without seeking external funding. Bootstrapping is an attractive option for entrepreneurs who want to maintain control over their business and avoid giving up equity.

Pros:
- You maintain control over your business
- You don't have to give up equity
- You have full creative freedom and can run your business as you see fit

Cons:
- You may have limited financial resources
- It can take longer to reach your business goals
- You may have to work a full-time job while growing your business

Angel Investors:
Angel investors are high-net-worth individuals who invest in startups and small businesses in exchange for equity. They can provide a significant amount of funding to help get your business off the ground.

Pros:
- Angel investors can provide a significant amount of funding
- They often have valuable industry connections and can provide guidance and mentorship
- They are willing to take risks on early-stage startups

Cons:
- Angel investors may require a significant amount of equity in exchange for their investment
- They may have a hands-on approach and want to be involved in the day-to-day operations of the business
- They may have different goals and priorities than the entrepreneur

Venture Capitalists:
Venture capitalists are investors who provide funding to startups and small businesses in exchange for equity. They typically invest in businesses that have a high growth potential and are in the early stages of development.

Pros:
- Venture capitalists can provide a significant amount of funding
- They often have valuable industry connections and can provide guidance and mentorship
- They are willing to take risks on early-stage startups

Cons:
- Venture capitalists may require a significant amount of equity in exchange for their investment

- They may have a hands-on approach and want to be involved in the day-to-day operations of the business
- They may have different goals and priorities than the entrepreneur

Crowdfunding:
1. Crowdfunding is the process of raising funds from a large number of people, usually through an online platform. This type of funding has become increasingly popular in recent years, as it allows entrepreneurs to tap into a large pool of potential investors.

Pros:
- Crowdfunding can provide a significant amount of funding
- It can help to validate the entrepreneur's idea
- It can create a community of supporters who are invested in the success of the business

Cons:
- Crowdfunding can be time-consuming and requires a significant amount of effort to launch and manage
- There is no guarantee that the funding goal will be met
- The entrepreneur may have to give up a portion of their equity or offer rewards to investors in exchange for their investment

Small Business Administration (SBA) Loans:
SBA loans are loans that are guaranteed by the U.S. Small Business Administration. These loans are provided by banks and other lending institutions and can be used for a variety of business purposes, including starting a new business, expanding an existing business, or purchasing equipment or inventory.

Pros:
- Low-interest rates on loans.
- Access to free business counseling and education.
- Loan options for businesses that may not qualify for traditional financing.

Cons:
- Lengthy application process and paperwork.
- Strict eligibility requirements.
- Limited loan amounts compared to other lenders.

III. **Preparing for Funding**

entrepreneurs seeking funding. Investors are more likely to invest in a business if they have a personal connection with the entrepreneur and believe in their vision.

To build relationships with potential investors, it's important to attend networking events, pitch competitions, and industry conferences where investors are likely to be present. It's also essential to research potential investors and their investment criteria before reaching out to them. This will help entrepreneurs determine which investors are the best fit for their business and tailor their pitch accordingly.

Entrepreneurs should also focus on building credibility and trust with potential investors. This can be done by demonstrating a deep understanding of the market and the competition, as well as by showing a track record of success. It's also important to be transparent and honest about the business and its potential risks.

Additionally, entrepreneurs should focus on building relationships with potential investors before they need funding. This means building relationships early and staying in touch with investors over time, even if they are not currently seeking funding.

- **Use online platforms**: There are a variety of online platforms that can help you connect with investors, such as AngelList, Gust, and SeedInvest. These platforms allow you to create a profile for your business, showcase your pitch deck, and connect with potential investors.
- **Consider your industry**: Different industries have different types of investors. For example, if you're in the tech industry, you may want to seek out venture capitalists or angel investors who specialize in tech startups. If you're in the food and beverage industry, you may want to seek out investors who have experience in that space.
- **Be prepared for due diligence**: Once you start meeting with potential investors, be prepared for due diligence. This means they will want to see your financials, your business plan, and your legal documentation. Make sure you have everything in order before you start pitching to investors.
- **Build relationships**: Building relationships with investors is key to securing funding. Investors want to invest in people they trust and believe in. Make sure to follow up after meetings, keep investors updated on your progress, and ask for feedback. Even if an investor decides not to invest in your business, they may be able to refer you to someone who will.

Pitching Your Business to Potential Investors:

Pitching your business to potential investors is an essential part of securing funding. A pitch is essentially a presentation that highlights the strengths and potential of your business to investors. It is an opportunity to communicate your vision, business model, and growth strategy to investors and convince them to invest in your venture.

Here are some tips on how to pitch your business effectively:
- **Start with a hook**: The first few seconds of your pitch are critical. You need to grab the investors' attention and make them interested in hearing more. Start with a hook that captures their attention and makes them want to know more.
- **Know your audience**: Before pitching to investors, research their investment interests and strategies. Tailor your pitch to their investment thesis and explain how your business fits into their portfolio.
- **Keep it simple:** Your pitch should be concise and easy to understand. Avoid using jargon or technical language that may confuse investors. Focus on explaining your business in simple terms and highlight the key benefits and unique features.
- **Highlight your team**: Investors are not just investing in your business; they are investing in your team. Highlight the strengths and experience of your team and explain how their skills will contribute to the success of your business.
- **Focus on traction**: Investors want to see evidence that your business has potential and is making progress. Highlight any traction, such as customer growth, revenue, or partnerships, to demonstrate that your business is gaining momentum.
- **Be transparent:** Investors want to know the risks and challenges associated with your business. Be transparent about the potential risks and explain how you plan to mitigate them.
- **Have a clear ask**: Your pitch should end with a clear ask. Specify the amount of funding you are looking for and explain how you plan to use the funds to grow your business.

In summary, pitching your business to potential investors is an essential step in securing funding for your business. It is crucial to tailor your pitch to your audience, keep it simple and concise, highlight your team's strengths, focus on traction, be transparent, and end with a clear ask. By following these tips, you can effectively communicate your business's potential and secure the funding you need to grow your business.

V. Negotiating and Closing the Deal

Obtaining funding for your business is not just about finding investors; it's also about negotiating and closing the deal. Negotiation is an art that requires practice and patience. In this section, we will discuss the negotiation process, tips for negotiating with investors, preparing for due diligence, and closing the deal.

Understanding the Negotiation Process:
The negotiation process is a critical stage in the funding process. It involves back-and-forth discussions between the investor and the entrepreneur to come up with a mutually beneficial agreement. The negotiation process may take several rounds and may include discussions on the terms and conditions of the investment, the percentage of ownership, and the rights and responsibilities of the investor.

Tips for Negotiating with Investors:

- **Know your worth**: Before entering into negotiations, it's crucial to know the value of your business and the amount of funding you need.
- **Keep emotions in check**: Negotiations can be emotional, but it's essential to keep your emotions in check to avoid making hasty decisions.
- **Focus on the long-term**: Negotiations should not just focus on the short-term benefits but should also consider the long-term implications of the deal.

Preparing for Due Diligence:
Due diligence is the process by which the investor verifies the entrepreneur's claims and checks the financial, legal, and operational aspects of the business. Before closing the deal, entrepreneurs must be prepared for the due diligence process. This includes having all the necessary documents and records ready for inspection, such as financial statements, legal documents, and business plans.

Closing the Deal:
Closing the deal is the final stage of the funding process. Once negotiations are complete, and due diligence is satisfactory, the entrepreneur and investor sign the agreement. It's essential to ensure that all terms and conditions agreed upon during negotiations are clearly outlined in the agreement. The entrepreneur should also be prepared to receive the funds, follow up with the investor, and maintain a positive relationship.

In conclusion, finding the right investors, building relationships, and negotiating and closing the deal is an intricate process. The key to success is being prepared, having a clear understanding of the negotiation process, and focusing on building long-term relationships with investors. With these skills and knowledge, entrepreneurs can successfully secure the funding they need to take their business to the next level.

VI. Alternative Funding Sources

In addition to traditional funding sources, there are alternative options for entrepreneurs to explore when seeking funding for their businesses. While these sources may not be suitable for every business, they can be a valuable option for those who are struggling to secure funding through traditional channels.

In this section, we will explore some of the most popular alternative funding sources, including crowdfunding, grants, and loans.

A. **Crowdfunding**

Crowdfunding has become an increasingly popular way for entrepreneurs to raise money for their business ventures. Crowdfunding is a process whereby entrepreneurs can pitch their business idea to a large group of people through an online platform. These individuals can then decide to invest in the business, often in exchange for equity in the company or a reward, such as a pre-order of the product.

One of the biggest benefits of crowdfunding is that it allows entrepreneurs to raise money without giving up equity in their company. This can be particularly attractive for those who are not willing to give up control of their business or dilute their ownership stake. Additionally, crowdfunding can help entrepreneurs to validate their business idea and generate buzz around their product or service.

However, there are also some downsides to crowdfunding. Crowdfunding campaigns can be time-consuming and require a significant amount of effort to successfully execute. Furthermore, entrepreneurs may not always be able to raise the full amount they are seeking through crowdfunding, and they may be required to deliver on rewards promised to backers, which can be expensive and time-consuming.

B. **Grants**

Grants are another alternative funding source that entrepreneurs may want to consider. Unlike loans, grants do not need to be paid back, which can be a major advantage for entrepreneurs who are struggling to secure traditional financing. Grants are often awarded by government agencies, nonprofit organizations, and corporations to support a particular cause or initiative.

One of the major benefits of grants is that they do not require entrepreneurs to take on debt, which can be particularly attractive for those who are already carrying a significant amount of debt or who have a low credit score. Additionally, grants can provide entrepreneurs with a significant amount of funding that can help them to grow their business quickly. However, grants can be difficult to obtain, and the application process can be time-consuming and require a significant amount of effort. Additionally, entrepreneurs may be required to use the funds for a specific purpose, which can limit their flexibility in terms of how they use the money.

C. **Loans**

Finally, loans are another alternative funding source that entrepreneurs can consider. While loans are not as attractive as grants or crowdfunding, they can be a valuable option for those who need to borrow money to fund their business. Loans are typically offered by banks, credit unions, and other financial institutions.

One of the biggest benefits of loans is that they provide entrepreneurs with a lump sum of money that they can use to grow their business. Additionally, loans can help entrepreneurs to build their credit score, which can be important for securing future financing. Finally, loans can be a flexible option for entrepreneurs, as they can choose from a variety of repayment terms and interest rates.

However, there are also some downsides to loans. Most loans require entrepreneurs to pay interest, which can be expensive over time. Additionally, loans can be difficult to qualify for, particularly for entrepreneurs who have a low credit score or who are new to business ownership. Finally, loans can be risky, as entrepreneurs are required to repay the loan even if their business does not succeed.

In conclusion, alternative funding sources can be a valuable option for entrepreneurs who are struggling to secure traditional financing. While each of these options has its own pros and cons, entrepreneurs should carefully consider which option is best for their particular situation. By doing so, they can increase their chances of securing the funding they need to grow their business and achieve their goals.

VII. Case Studies

One of the most effective ways to learn about funding strategies is by studying successful and unsuccessful funding attempts of others. In this section, we will examine a few case studies of companies that have gone through the funding process and what we can learn from their experiences.

Case Study 1: Uber

Uber is a ride-hailing company that has revolutionized the transportation industry. The company has raised over $25 billion in funding to date. Uber's funding rounds have been very successful due to their innovative business model and strong growth potential. The company has been able to attract investors who are willing to invest in their vision of the future of transportation.

Lessons Learned:
1. **Have a clear vision**: Uber's founders had a clear vision of what they wanted to achieve, and they were able to articulate it effectively to potential investors.
2. **Build a strong team**: Uber's founders were able to build a team of experienced and talented individuals who were able to execute their vision effectively.
3. **Disrupt an industry**: Uber was able to disrupt the traditional taxi industry by providing a better and more convenient service, which helped them attract investors.

Case Study 2: Theranos

Theranos was a healthcare startup that promised to revolutionize the blood testing industry. The company raised over $700 million in funding from prominent investors. However, the company was later found to have made false claims about their technology, and their founder, Elizabeth Holmes, is now facing criminal charges.

Lessons Learned:

1. **Be transparent**: It is important to be transparent with investors about the technology and products being developed and to avoid making false claims.
2. **Have a solid product**: Investors want to see a solid product before investing in a company. It is important to thoroughly test and validate the product before presenting it to investors.
3. **Build trust**: Investors need to trust the company and its leadership. Building trust takes time and effort, but it is essential for successful fundraising.

Case Study 3: Pebble

Pebble was a smartwatch company that raised over $10 million on Kickstarter. The company was able to generate a lot of buzz due to its innovative product, and it was eventually acquired by Fitbit.

Lessons Learned:

1. **Have a unique product**: Pebble was able to attract a large number of backers on Kickstarter because they had a unique and innovative product.
2. **Leverage crowdfunding**: Crowdfunding can be a powerful tool for startups to raise funds and generate buzz around their products.
3. **Be open to acquisition**: Startups should be open to the possibility of being acquired, as it can be a good exit strategy for investors and founders.

Conclusion:
In conclusion, studying successful and unsuccessful funding attempts can help entrepreneurs learn valuable lessons about how to approach fundraising. Building a strong team, having a clear vision, and disrupting an industry are some of the factors that can contribute to successful fundraising. Transparency, a solid product, and building trust are also essential. Finally, leveraging alternative funding sources and being open to acquisition can also be useful strategies for startups.

VIII. Conclusion

Chapter 5 of "Hustle Harder: How to Dominate the Game and Crush Your Competition" concludes with an overview of the chapter's key points, a final encouragement for readers to hustle for funding, and concluding thoughts from the author. Recapping the chapter's main ideas, finding the right investors for a business is a critical component of obtaining funding. Building relationships with potential investors is key to developing trust and securing their support. Pitching a business to investors requires careful planning and execution, and due diligence is crucial in preparing for negotiations and closing the deal. Alternative funding sources, such as crowdfunding, grants, and loans, are also viable options for entrepreneurs.

In conclusion, the chapter emphasizes the importance of being resourceful and persistent when seeking funding for a business. The author encourages readers to continue hustling and exploring different funding sources, highlighting the fact that funding is often the lifeblood of a business and essential for achieving success. Ultimately, the chapter concludes with the author's final thoughts on the topic and a call to action for readers to continue striving towards their entrepreneurial goals with tenacity and resilience.

"The only thing standing between you and your goal is the story you keep telling yourself as to why you can't achieve it"

- Jordan Belfort

Chapter 6: Building Your Dream Team

I. **Introduction**
- Explanation of why building a strong team is critical to business success
- Overview of what will be covered in the chapter

II. **Identifying the key roles and skills needed for your business**
- Discussion of how to determine which positions are necessary for your business to thrive
- Tips for identifying the necessary skills and qualities for each role
- Examples of common positions for startups and small businesses

III. **Hiring, training, and managing employees and contractors**
- Strategies for recruiting and hiring the best candidates
- Tips for onboarding and training new employees
- Best practices for managing and retaining employees and contractors
- Discussion of legal considerations, such as labor laws and contracts

IV. **Fostering a culture of innovation, collaboration, and accountability**
- Explanation of why company culture is important and how it affects productivity and morale
- Tips for creating a positive work environment and promoting innovation
- Discussion of effective communication strategies and team-building activities
- Best practices for establishing accountability and promoting individual and team success

V. Case studies
- Analysis of successful team-building strategies and lessons learned from failures
- Examples of businesses with strong and effective teams
- Discussion of how different industries and business models impact team building

VI. Conclusion
- Recap of key points and strategies for building your dream team
- Encouragement to prioritize team building and create a culture of success
- Final thoughts from the author on the importance of a strong team and how it contributes to overall success.

Chapter 6: Building Your Dream Team

In today's fast-paced business world, the importance of building a strong and effective team cannot be overstated. The success or failure of any business venture depends heavily on the quality of the team behind it. As a business owner or entrepreneur, it is important to recognize that you cannot do everything yourself, and you will need a team of skilled individuals to help you bring your vision to life.

Building a dream team is not an easy task, but it is a necessary one. A strong team can help you to achieve your goals faster and more efficiently than you could on your own. In this chapter, we will explore the various aspects of building a dream team, including identifying the key roles and skills needed for your business, hiring, training, and managing employees and contractors, and fostering a culture of innovation, collaboration, and accountability.

The first step in building your dream team is to understand the critical roles and skills that you will need to make your business successful. These may include sales and marketing, product development, finance and accounting, customer service, and operations, among others. Each role will require specific skills, such as leadership, communication, problem-solving, and technical expertise. It is important to identify these roles and the skills needed to fulfill them early on in the process, so that you can start building your team with intention.

Once you have identified the roles and skills needed for your business, the next step is to start the hiring process.

This involves creating job descriptions, sourcing candidates, and conducting interviews. It is important to be clear about the qualifications and experience required for each role, and to look for candidates who not only have the technical skills you need but also share your values and vision for the business.

Hiring is only the first step, however. Once you have brought new team members on board, it is important to train and manage them effectively. This includes setting clear expectations, providing ongoing feedback, and creating a culture of accountability. It is also important to ensure that all team members have the resources and support they need to do their jobs effectively.

Finally, building a dream team requires fostering a culture of innovation, collaboration, and accountability. This means creating an environment where team members feel comfortable sharing their ideas and opinions, working together to solve problems, and holding themselves and each other accountable for their work. By creating a culture that values these qualities, you can help to ensure that your team is motivated, engaged, and focused on achieving your business goals.

In conclusion, building a dream team is critical to the success of any business venture. By identifying the key roles and skills needed for your business, hiring, training, and managing employees and contractors effectively, and fostering a culture of innovation, collaboration, and accountability, you can create a team that is capable of achieving great things. In the following sections of this chapter, we will explore each of these aspects of building a dream team in more detail, providing you with the tools and insights you need to make it happen.

Building a dream team is one of the most important aspects of creating and growing a successful business. The right people with the right skills can make all the difference in the world.

However, identifying the key roles and skills needed for your business can be a daunting task, especially for startups and small businesses. In this section, we will discuss how to determine which positions are necessary for your business to thrive, tips for identifying the necessary skills and qualities for each role, and provide examples of common positions for startups and small businesses.

The first step in identifying the key roles and skills needed for your business is to understand your business goals and objectives. This includes analyzing the current state of your business, identifying potential areas of growth, and determining the resources necessary to achieve your goals. By having a clear understanding of your business needs, you can create a comprehensive list of positions that are critical to achieving your objectives.

Once you have a list of positions, the next step is to identify the necessary skills and qualities for each role. This includes hard skills, such as technical expertise, as well as soft skills, such as communication and teamwork. To identify the necessary skills and qualities, consider the responsibilities and expectations for each role, and create a list of skills and qualities that would enable someone to be successful in that position. Additionally, it is important to consider the culture of your business and the values that you want your team to embody.

Here are some tips for identifying the key roles and skills needed for your business:
- Analyze your business goals and objectives to determine the resources necessary to achieve them.
- Create a comprehensive list of positions critical to achieving your business objectives.
- Identify the necessary hard and soft skills and qualities for each role.

- Consider the culture of your business and the values that you want your team to embody.
- Be flexible and adaptable to changes in your business needs, and be willing to adjust your team structure as necessary.

Some common positions for startups and small businesses include:

- **Founder/CEO**: responsible for overall business strategy and growth.
- **Marketing Manager**: responsible for developing and executing marketing campaigns.
- **Sales Manager**: responsible for generating sales and revenue for the business.
- **Operations Manager**: responsible for managing day-to-day operations of the business.
- **Finance Manager**: responsible for managing the finances of the business, including budgeting and forecasting.
- **Customer Service Representative**: responsible for providing excellent customer service and support.
- **Technical Lead**: responsible for leading the development of technical products and services.

In conclusion, identifying the key roles and skills needed for your business is critical to building a strong and successful team. By analyzing your business goals and objectives, creating a comprehensive list of positions, and identifying the necessary skills and qualities for each role, you can build a team that will help your business thrive. Remember to be flexible and adaptable to changes in your business needs, and be willing to adjust your team structure as necessary.

Building a strong team is not just about hiring the best candidates, but also about retaining them and ensuring they remain motivated and engaged. This is where effective management practices come into play.

In this section, we will discuss some of the best practices for managing and retaining employees and contractors.

- **Clear Communication**: Communication is key to any successful relationship, and the relationship between an employer and employee is no exception. Employers should make sure to establish clear communication channels with their employees and contractors, including regular check-ins and open-door policies. This helps to build trust and fosters a sense of transparency and honesty.
- **Goal Setting and Feedback**: Employees and contractors need to understand what is expected of them and how their performance will be evaluated. Setting clear goals and providing regular feedback on progress is an effective way to keep employees engaged and motivated. This also helps to identify areas for improvement and opportunities for professional development.
- **Flexibility**: The modern workforce values flexibility and work-life balance. Employers who offer flexible work arrangements, such as remote work, flexible hours, or job sharing, are more likely to attract and retain top talent. Flexibility also helps to accommodate different needs and schedules, which can lead to increased job satisfaction and reduced turnover.
- **Recognition and Rewards**: Employees and contractors who feel valued and appreciated are more likely to stay with an organization. Employers can recognize their employees' hard work and contributions through formal and informal recognition programs, such as bonuses, promotions, or public praise. Rewards also help to foster a sense of healthy competition and encourage employees to strive for excellence.

- **Training and Development**: Providing opportunities for training and development is critical to retaining top talent. Employers who invest in their employees' professional growth and development not only increase their value to the organization but also demonstrate a commitment to their employees' long-term success.
- **Labor Laws and Contracts**: Employers must comply with labor laws and regulations to avoid legal disputes and ensure a fair and safe working environment for their employees. This includes ensuring compliance with minimum wage and overtime laws, providing a safe workplace, and complying with anti-discrimination and anti-harassment laws. Employers should also have clear contracts in place that outline the terms of employment, including pay, benefits, and expectations.

In conclusion, building a strong team requires effective management practices that foster a culture of trust, engagement, and collaboration. Clear communication, goal setting and feedback, flexibility, recognition and rewards, training and development, and compliance with labor laws and contracts are all essential elements of effective management. Employers who invest in their employees' success and well-being are more likely to attract and retain top talent, which is critical to achieving long-term business success.

A strong company culture is essential for attracting and retaining top talent, improving productivity, and achieving long-term success. Creating a positive work environment and fostering a culture of innovation, collaboration, and accountability can help your business stand out and give your team the tools they need to thrive. In this section, we will explore some best practices for establishing a positive culture and promoting individual and team success.

- **Why company culture is important:** Company culture refers to the shared values, beliefs, attitudes, and behaviors that define how people work together in an organization. It sets the tone for how employees interact with each other, their clients, and their work. A positive company culture can help to attract and retain top talent, improve productivity, and foster innovation. On the other hand, a toxic or negative culture can lead to high turnover, low morale, and poor performance.
- **Tips for creating a positive work environment and promoting innovation:** To create a positive work environment, start by establishing a clear mission and values that align with your team's goals and objectives. Communicate these values clearly to your team and ensure that they are reflected in your day-to-day operations. Encourage open communication, collaboration, and creativity by creating opportunities for team members to share ideas, brainstorm, and work together on projects. Celebrate successes and milestones, and provide opportunities for professional growth and development.
- **Effective communication strategies and team-building activities:** Effective communication is key to building a positive culture. Ensure that your team members understand their roles and responsibilities and have the resources they need to succeed. Encourage open communication and feedback, and provide opportunities for team members to share their thoughts and ideas. Host regular team-building activities, such as company retreats, social events, and community service projects, to help build trust, camaraderie, and a sense of shared purpose.

- **Establishing accountability and promoting individual and team success:** To promote individual and team success, establish clear goals and metrics for performance, and provide regular feedback and coaching to help team members achieve these goals. Create a culture of accountability by setting expectations and holding team members responsible for meeting them. Celebrate successes and recognize team members who go above and beyond to contribute to the success of the company.

In conclusion, creating a positive work environment and fostering a culture of innovation, collaboration, and accountability can help your business stand out, attract and retain top talent, and achieve long-term success. By following these best practices, you can create a strong team that is motivated, engaged, and committed to achieving your business goals. Remember, building a dream team takes time, effort, and a commitment to ongoing improvement, but the rewards are well worth the investment.

Building a strong and effective team is critical to the success of any business, regardless of its size or industry. In this section, we will examine case studies of businesses that have successfully built strong teams and those that have failed to do so. By analyzing these case studies, we can gain valuable insights into the strategies that work and those that do not when it comes to team building.

Analysis of successful team-building strategies:
Netflix:
Netflix is a great example of a company that has built a strong team. One of the key strategies that Netflix uses is to hire only high-performing employees who are able to work independently and have a track record of delivering results.

This allows the company to avoid micromanagement and focus on building a culture of innovation and creativity.

Another strategy that Netflix uses is to create a culture of freedom and responsibility. This means that employees are given the freedom to make decisions and take risks, but they are also held accountable for their actions. This approach has helped Netflix to attract and retain top talent, resulting in a highly productive and successful team.

Zappos:

Zappos is another company that has built a strong team. One of the key strategies that Zappos uses is to create a strong company culture that emphasizes customer service and employee happiness. This culture is reinforced through regular team-building activities, such as company-wide events and volunteer opportunities.

Zappos also places a strong emphasis on hiring for cultural fit. The company believes that it is more important to hire employees who share the company's values and beliefs than those who simply have the necessary skills and experience. By hiring employees who are a good fit for the company culture, Zappos has been able to create a highly engaged and motivated team.

Lessons learned from failures:

Enron:

Enron is a company that famously failed due to a toxic culture that was focused on short-term gain rather than long-term success. The company placed too much emphasis on financial results and did not foster a culture of ethics and accountability. Enron's leaders also failed to hire and promote based on merit and instead favored those who were willing to engage in unethical and illegal behavior. This led to a team that was focused on personal gain rather than the success of the company as a whole.

Uber:
Uber is another company that has faced criticism for its toxic culture. The company has been accused of fostering a culture of sexism, harassment, and discrimination. This has resulted in a high rate of employee turnover and a negative public image. Uber's leaders have also been criticized for their focus on growth at all costs, which has resulted in a lack of accountability and a disregard for ethical behavior. As a result, the company has struggled to build a strong and effective team.

Examples of businesses with strong and effective teams:

Google:
Google is known for having one of the best teams in the tech industry. The company places a strong emphasis on hiring only the best talent and creating a culture of innovation and collaboration. Google also encourages employees to take risks and think outside the box.

To foster a culture of innovation and collaboration, Google provides employees with a range of perks, including free food, on-site massages, and even nap pods. These perks help to create a positive work environment that encourages creativity and productivity.

Southwest Airlines:
Southwest Airlines is a prime example of a company with a strong and effective team. The company's success can be attributed to its unique approach to team building, which involves hiring for personality and attitude rather than just experience and skills. The company also encourages collaboration and open communication among team members, resulting in a positive work environment and excellent customer service. This has resulted in Southwest Airlines consistently ranking among the top airlines in the industry in terms of customer satisfaction and employee engagement.

Another important aspect of team building is recognizing and rewarding employees for their hard work and achievements. This can be done through bonuses, promotions, or even simple gestures such as a public acknowledgment or a thank-you note. By doing so, you show your employees that their efforts are valued and that their work is contributing to the success of the business.

Furthermore, it is essential to establish a culture of trust and transparency within the team. Encourage open communication and create a safe space for employees to voice their opinions and concerns. This not only fosters innovation and creativity but also helps to prevent misunderstandings and conflicts.

Lastly, it is crucial to remember that team building is an ongoing process. As the business evolves and grows, so should the team. Regular check-ins and evaluations can help identify areas of improvement and provide opportunities for continued learning and development.

In conclusion, building a dream team is a crucial aspect of achieving business success, and this chapter provides a comprehensive guide on how to achieve this goal. From identifying the key roles and skills required for a business to thrive to creating a positive work culture, the chapter offers valuable insights and tips for entrepreneurs and business owners. Furthermore, the analysis of successful team-building strategies and lessons learned from failures, as well as examples of businesses with strong and effective teams, provide inspiration and guidance for those looking to improve their team-building skills. Additionally, the discussion of how different industries and business models impact team building is a reminder that there is no one-size-fits-all approach to building a successful team. Overall, this chapter provides a wealth of knowledge and practical advice for anyone looking to build a strong and effective team.

In this chapter, we have discussed the importance of building a strong and effective team for the success of your business. A team that works together towards a common goal and has a positive culture can make all the difference in achieving your business objectives. We have covered the following key points and strategies for building your dream team:

- **Introduction**: We started by discussing why building a strong team is critical to business success. We explained how a well-functioning team can help you achieve your goals and beat the competition.
- **Identifying the key roles and skills needed for your business**: We talked about the importance of determining the necessary positions and skills for your business to thrive. We provided tips for identifying the essential qualities and skills for each role and gave examples of common positions for startups and small businesses.
- **Hiring, training, and managing employees and contractors**: We discussed strategies for recruiting and hiring the best candidates, tips for onboarding and training new employees, best practices for managing and retaining employees and contractors, and legal considerations such as labor laws and contracts.
- **Fostering a culture of innovation, collaboration, and accountability**: We explained why company culture is important and how it affects productivity and morale. We provided tips for creating a positive work environment, promoting innovation, effective communication strategies, and team-building activities. We also discussed the best practices for establishing accountability and promoting individual and team success.

- **Case studies**: We analyzed successful team-building strategies and lessons learned from failures. We gave examples of businesses with strong and effective teams and discussed how different industries and business models impact team building.

Encouragement to prioritize team building and create a culture of success

Building your dream team takes time, effort, and dedication. It is not an easy task, but it is necessary for the success of your business. As a leader, you should prioritize team building and create a culture of success that encourages your team to work towards a common goal. Remember, a positive work environment, effective communication, and accountability are the keys to building a strong and effective team.

Final thoughts from the author on the importance of a strong team and how it contributes to overall success.

In conclusion, building your dream team is one of the most important tasks you will undertake as a business owner or leader. A well-functioning team can make all the difference in achieving your business objectives and beating the competition. Remember to prioritize team building, create a positive work environment, and establish accountability to promote individual and team success. With these strategies in place, you can build a strong and effective team that will take your business to the next level. Good luck on your journey towards building your dream team!

"Coming together is a beginning. Keeping together is progress. Working together is success."

- Henry Ford

Chapter 7: Scaling Up

I. **Introduction**
- Explanation of what scaling up means in the context of a business
- Importance of scaling up for achieving long-term growth and success
- Overview of the topics covered in the chapter

II. **Understanding the challenges and opportunities of scaling your business**
- Discussion of common challenges businesses face when scaling up
- Tips for overcoming those challenges and taking advantage of opportunities
- Examples of successful businesses that have scaled up and how they did it

III. **Developing systems and processes to streamline operations**
- Importance of creating efficient and effective systems and processes for scaling up
- Tips for identifying areas that need improvement and implementing changes
- Examples of businesses that have successfully streamlined their operations and scaled up as a result

IV. **Expanding your product/service offerings and markets**
- Explanation of the benefits of expanding your offerings and markets when scaling up
- Tips for researching and identifying new markets and opportunities
- Examples of businesses that have successfully expanded their product/service offerings and markets

V. Overcoming the challenges of scaling up
- Discussion of the most common challenges businesses face when scaling up and how to overcome them
- Tips for managing growth and maintaining quality during the scaling up process
- Examples of businesses that have faced and overcome challenges when scaling up

VI. Conclusion
- Recap of key points and strategies for scaling up a business
- Encouragement to prioritize scaling up for long-term growth and success
- Final thoughts from the author on the importance of scaling up and how it contributes to overall success.

Chapter 7: Scaling Up

I. Introduction

As a business owner, you likely have big ambitions for your company's growth and success. However, scaling up your business can be a daunting task, with many challenges and obstacles to overcome. In this chapter, we will discuss what scaling up means in the context of a business, why it is important for achieving long-term growth and success, and provide an overview of the topics covered in this chapter.

Scaling up is the process of increasing the size, reach, and scope of your business operations to achieve long-term growth and success. This can include expanding your customer base, developing new products or services, entering new markets, and increasing revenue and profitability. While scaling up can be challenging, it is an essential part of building a successful and sustainable business.

One of the main reasons why scaling up is important is that it allows you to take advantage of new opportunities and stay ahead of your competition. By expanding your business, you can tap into new markets, offer new products or services, and reach more customers. This can help you to increase revenue, build brand recognition, and establish yourself as a market leader.

Another important reason why scaling up is important is that it can help you to achieve long-term financial stability and sustainability. By growing your business, you can increase your profitability and create more opportunities for reinvestment in your company.

This can help you to weather economic downturns, invest in new technologies or systems, and build a stronger foundation for future growth.

In this chapter, we will cover a range of topics related to scaling up your business, including developing systems and processes to streamline operations, expanding your product and service offerings, and entering new markets. By following the strategies and tips outlined in this chapter, you can position your business for long-term success and growth.

II. Understanding the challenges and opportunities of scaling your business

Scaling up a business can be both an exciting and daunting prospect. On one hand, expanding operations can bring in more revenue, reach new markets, and increase brand recognition. On the other hand, it requires a lot of planning, resources, and can pose various challenges. In this section, we will explore some of the common challenges and opportunities that businesses may encounter when scaling up.

One of the biggest challenges in scaling up is managing cash flow. Expanding a business requires investment in equipment, technology, and personnel, all of which require upfront costs. It is essential to have a solid financial plan that takes into account all the costs associated with scaling up and ensures adequate funding is available. A business owner may also need to consider obtaining financing from investors or banks to cover the initial costs.

Another challenge is maintaining the quality of products and services as the business expands. With growth comes the need for increased production and delivery, and it can be difficult to ensure consistency in quality. To overcome this challenge, businesses should develop and implement standardized procedures for all aspects of the production process.

This will ensure that quality remains consistent and that the customer experience remains positive.

Additionally, managing human resources becomes more challenging when scaling up. As the business grows, the workforce will likely expand, which can be difficult to manage. It is essential to have strong HR policies in place to recruit, train, and retain talented employees. Creating a positive work culture that promotes teamwork and accountability is also crucial for success.

Despite these challenges, scaling up also presents many opportunities. For example, expanding into new markets can increase brand recognition and bring in new revenue streams. Adding new products or services can also diversify a business's offerings and appeal to a broader customer base. Furthermore, scaling up can lead to increased efficiency and productivity through the development of standardized procedures and automation of certain tasks.

Many successful businesses have overcome these challenges and taken advantage of the opportunities presented by scaling up. One such example is Netflix, which started as a DVD rental service but evolved into a streaming giant, now available in over 190 countries worldwide. Netflix was able to successfully scale up by investing in technology, offering a wide range of original content, and expanding its offerings to different markets.

In conclusion, scaling up a business requires careful planning, dedication, and a willingness to overcome the challenges that come with growth. By understanding these challenges and opportunities, business owners can develop strategies that will help them navigate the process successfully. With the right approach and mindset, scaling up can bring significant rewards, including increased revenue, brand recognition, and long-term success.

III. **Developing systems and processes to streamline operations**

As businesses grow, they often encounter various challenges that can hinder their growth and success. One of the main challenges businesses face is keeping up with the increasing demand for their products or services while maintaining the quality and efficiency of their operations. This is where developing systems and processes comes into play.

Developing effective systems and processes is essential for scaling up a business. These systems and processes enable businesses to operate more efficiently, reduce costs, and improve their overall productivity. By streamlining operations, businesses can save time and resources, which can be reinvested in other areas of the business, such as marketing or product development.

To develop effective systems and processes, businesses need to start by identifying areas that need improvement. This may involve analyzing the current processes and identifying bottlenecks or areas that are inefficient. Once these areas are identified, businesses can then develop and implement new processes that are more efficient and effective.

One example of a business that has successfully streamlined its operations is Amazon. From its early days as an online bookstore, Amazon has continuously worked to improve its processes and systems. The company has invested heavily in automation, which has enabled it to reduce its operational costs and offer faster and more reliable delivery to its customers. Amazon's focus on operational efficiency has been a key factor in its success and has enabled it to expand into new markets and product categories.

Another example of a business that has successfully streamlined its operations is McDonald's. The fast-food giant has developed a highly efficient and standardized process for preparing and serving its food.

This process has enabled McDonald's to offer consistent quality across all its locations and has contributed to the company's global success.

In conclusion, developing systems and processes to streamline operations is essential for scaling up a business. By identifying areas that need improvement and implementing new processes that are more efficient and effective, businesses can reduce costs, save time, and improve their overall productivity. Examples of successful businesses such as Amazon and McDonald's demonstrate the importance of operational efficiency in achieving long-term growth and success.

IV. **Expanding your product/service offerings and markets**

Expanding your product/service offerings and markets is an important strategy for scaling up your business. It allows you to reach a wider audience and generate more revenue. However, it also comes with its own set of challenges and risks. In this section, we will discuss the benefits of expanding your offerings and markets and provide tips for researching and identifying new opportunities.

Benefits of expanding your offerings and markets:

1. **Increased revenue**: Expanding your offerings and markets allows you to reach a larger audience and generate more revenue. This can help you achieve long-term growth and success.
2. **Competitive advantage**: By expanding your offerings and markets, you can gain a competitive advantage over other businesses in your industry. This can help you attract new customers and retain existing ones.
3. **Diversification**: Expanding your offerings and markets can help you diversify your revenue streams, reducing your reliance on a single product or market.

Tips for researching and identifying new opportunities:
- **Conduct market research**: Before expanding your offerings and markets, it is important to conduct market research to identify new opportunities. This can include analyzing market trends, customer needs, and competitor offerings.
- **Develop a plan**: Once you have identified new opportunities, develop a plan for how you will expand your offerings and markets. This should include setting goals, defining your target audience, and developing a marketing strategy.
- **Test the market**: Before fully committing to an expansion, test the market to see if there is demand for your product or service. This can include conducting focus groups, surveys, or pilot programs.

Examples of businesses that have successfully expanded their product/service offerings and markets:
- **Amazon**: Amazon started as an online bookstore but has since expanded to sell a wide range of products, including electronics, clothing, and home goods. They have also expanded their market by offering their services internationally.
- **Netflix**: Netflix started as a DVD-by-mail rental service but has since expanded to a streaming service, producing its own original content, and expanding its market to other countries.
- **Apple**: Apple started as a computer company but has since expanded to offer a wide range of products, including smartphones, tablets, and smartwatches. They have also expanded their market by offering their products in countries around the world.

In conclusion, expanding your product/service offerings and markets is an important strategy for scaling up your business.

Tips for researching and identifying new opportunities:
- **Conduct market research**: Before expanding your offerings and markets, it is important to conduct market research to identify new opportunities. This can include analyzing market trends, customer needs, and competitor offerings.
- **Develop a plan**: Once you have identified new opportunities, develop a plan for how you will expand your offerings and markets. This should include setting goals, defining your target audience, and developing a marketing strategy.
- **Test the market**: Before fully committing to an expansion, test the market to see if there is demand for your product or service. This can include conducting focus groups, surveys, or pilot programs.

Examples of businesses that have successfully expanded their product/service offerings and markets:
- **Amazon**: Amazon started as an online bookstore but has since expanded to sell a wide range of products, including electronics, clothing, and home goods. They have also expanded their market by offering their services internationally.
- **Netflix**: Netflix started as a DVD-by-mail rental service but has since expanded to a streaming service, producing its own original content, and expanding its market to other countries.
- **Apple**: Apple started as a computer company but has since expanded to offer a wide range of products, including smartphones, tablets, and smartwatches. They have also expanded their market by offering their products in countries around the world.

In conclusion, expanding your product/service offerings and markets is an important strategy for scaling up your business.

Tips for researching and identifying new opportunities:
- **Conduct market research**: Before expanding your offerings and markets, it is important to conduct market research to identify new opportunities. This can include analyzing market trends, customer needs, and competitor offerings.
- **Develop a plan**: Once you have identified new opportunities, develop a plan for how you will expand your offerings and markets. This should include setting goals, defining your target audience, and developing a marketing strategy.
- **Test the market**: Before fully committing to an expansion, test the market to see if there is demand for your product or service. This can include conducting focus groups, surveys, or pilot programs.

Examples of businesses that have successfully expanded their product/service offerings and markets:
- **Amazon**: Amazon started as an online bookstore but has since expanded to sell a wide range of products, including electronics, clothing, and home goods. They have also expanded their market by offering their services internationally.
- **Netflix**: Netflix started as a DVD-by-mail rental service but has since expanded to a streaming service, producing its own original content, and expanding its market to other countries.
- **Apple**: Apple started as a computer company but has since expanded to offer a wide range of products, including smartphones, tablets, and smartwatches. They have also expanded their market by offering their products in countries around the world.

In conclusion, expanding your product/service offerings and markets is an important strategy for scaling up your business.

It can provide numerous benefits, including increased revenue, competitive advantage, and diversification. However, it is important to conduct market research, develop a plan, and test the market before fully committing to an expansion. By following these tips and learning from successful businesses that have expanded their offerings and markets, you can increase your chances of success and achieve long-term growth and success.

V. Overcoming the challenges of scaling up

Scaling up a business can be an exciting and challenging journey. While there are many benefits to expanding your operations, there are also significant challenges to overcome. In this section, we'll explore some of the most common challenges businesses face when scaling up and provide tips for overcoming them.

One of the biggest challenges when scaling up is maintaining quality while managing growth. As your business expands, it's essential to ensure that the quality of your products or services remains high. This can be a significant challenge, as it often requires changes to your operations, supply chain, and management processes.

To overcome this challenge, it's important to focus on creating scalable systems and processes that can handle increased demand while maintaining quality. This may require investments in technology, training, and hiring additional staff. It's also essential to monitor and track key performance indicators (KPIs) to ensure that quality standards are being met.

Another challenge when scaling up is managing cash flow. Expanding your operations often requires significant investments in equipment, inventory, and marketing.

It can provide numerous benefits, including increased revenue, competitive advantage, and diversification. However, it is important to conduct market research, develop a plan, and test the market before fully committing to an expansion. By following these tips and learning from successful businesses that have expanded their offerings and markets, you can increase your chances of success and achieve long-term growth and success.

V. Overcoming the challenges of scaling up

Scaling up a business can be an exciting and challenging journey. While there are many benefits to expanding your operations, there are also significant challenges to overcome. In this section, we'll explore some of the most common challenges businesses face when scaling up and provide tips for overcoming them.

One of the biggest challenges when scaling up is maintaining quality while managing growth. As your business expands, it's essential to ensure that the quality of your products or services remains high. This can be a significant challenge, as it often requires changes to your operations, supply chain, and management processes.

To overcome this challenge, it's important to focus on creating scalable systems and processes that can handle increased demand while maintaining quality. This may require investments in technology, training, and hiring additional staff. It's also essential to monitor and track key performance indicators (KPIs) to ensure that quality standards are being met.

Another challenge when scaling up is managing cash flow. Expanding your operations often requires significant investments in equipment, inventory, and marketing.

VI. Conclusion

Chapter 7 of "Hustle Harder: How to Dominate the Game and Crush Your Competition" focuses on scaling up a business. As we have discussed in this chapter, scaling up is crucial for achieving long-term growth and success. In this section, we will summarize the key points and strategies for scaling up a business and emphasize the importance of prioritizing this process.

To begin with, scaling up a business involves overcoming challenges and identifying opportunities for growth. It is essential to develop systems and processes that streamline operations and to expand your product/service offerings and markets. However, scaling up a business can be a challenging task, and you must be prepared to overcome the obstacles that come your way.

One of the main challenges that businesses face when scaling up is managing growth and maintaining quality. As you expand your business, you may face difficulties in managing cash flow, retaining employees, and maintaining customer satisfaction. Therefore, it is crucial to have a clear plan in place to address these challenges and to ensure that the quality of your product or service is not compromised.

Another significant challenge is identifying new markets and opportunities. You must conduct thorough research and analysis to understand your target audience and identify new opportunities for growth. You may also need to adapt your product or service to suit the needs of new markets.

To overcome these challenges, you need to be proactive and strategic in your approach. It is essential to have a growth mindset and to be willing to take calculated risks. You must also be open to learning from failures and adapting your strategies accordingly.

In conclusion, scaling up is a critical process for achieving long-term growth and success in business. By developing systems and processes, expanding your offerings and markets, and overcoming challenges, you can take your business to the next level. It is essential to prioritize scaling up and to have a clear plan in place for managing growth and maintaining quality. With the right mindset and strategies, you can achieve your goals and dominate the game.

"Don't watch the clock; do what it does. Keep going."

- Sam Levenson

Chapter 8: Crushing Your Competition

I. **Introduction**
- Explanation of the importance of crushing your competition in business
- Overview of the topics covered in the chapter

II. **Staying ahead of the game by innovating and adapting**
- Discussion of the benefits of innovation and adaptation in business
- Tips for identifying opportunities for innovation and adaptation
- Examples of businesses that have successfully stayed ahead of the game through innovation and adaptation

III. **Building a loyal customer base and reputation**
- Explanation of the benefits of a loyal customer base and good reputation in business
- Tips for building a loyal customer base and positive reputation
- Examples of businesses that have successfully built a loyal customer base and positive reputation

IV. **Maintaining a competitive edge through continuous learning and improvement**
- Discussion of the benefits of continuous learning and improvement in business
- Tips for identifying areas for improvement and implementing changes
- Examples of businesses that have successfully maintained a competitive edge through continuous learning and improvement

V. Overcoming challenges in crushing your competition
- Discussion of the most common challenges businesses face when trying to crush their competition and how to overcome them
- Tips for managing competition and maintaining focus on your own business
- Examples of businesses that have faced and overcome challenges in crushing their competition

VI. Conclusion
- Recap of key points and strategies for crushing your competition
- Encouragement to prioritize innovation, customer loyalty, and continuous learning and improvement for long-term success
- Final thoughts from the author on the importance of crushing your competition and how it contributes to overall success.

Chapter 8: Crushing Your Competition

I. Introduction

In the world of business, competition is inevitable. Every industry and market has its own set of players vying for the same customers and revenue. It can be tough to stand out and get noticed in a crowded market, but that's exactly what you need to do if you want to succeed. To dominate the game and achieve long-term success, you need to crush your competition. Crushing your competition doesn't necessarily mean putting them out of business. It's about outperforming them in every way possible, so you're the first choice for customers. This can be done by offering superior products or services, delivering exceptional customer service, and building a brand that resonates with people. By doing these things, you'll be able to capture more market share and leave your competition behind. The importance of crushing your competition cannot be overstated. If you don't actively work to beat your competitors, they will beat you. It's a simple fact of business. The companies that succeed are the ones that constantly strive to improve, innovate, and adapt to the ever-changing marketplace. Those that become complacent and fail to innovate will inevitably fall behind.

Throughout this chapter, we'll explore different strategies and tactics for crushing your competition. From staying ahead of the game by innovating and adapting, to building a loyal customer base and maintaining a competitive edge through continuous learning and improvement, we'll cover everything you need to know to stay ahead of the curve and come out on top.

In conclusion, scaling up is a critical process for achieving long-term growth and success in business. By developing systems and processes, expanding your offerings and markets, and overcoming challenges, you can take your business to the next level. It is essential to prioritize scaling up and to have a clear plan in place for managing growth and maintaining quality. With the right mindset and strategies, you can achieve your goals and dominate the game.

II. Staying ahead of the game by innovating and adapting

Innovation and adaptation are key factors in staying ahead of the competition in business. In today's ever-changing market, businesses that fail to innovate and adapt to new trends risk being left behind. Therefore, it is essential to continuously evaluate your business and identify opportunities for innovation and adaptation.

One of the primary benefits of innovation and adaptation is that it enables a business to differentiate itself from its competitors. By creating unique products, services, or processes, a business can stand out in a crowded market and attract customers who are looking for something new and exciting. This differentiation also creates a competitive advantage that can be difficult for other businesses to replicate, allowing the innovating company to maintain its position as an industry leader.

Innovation and adaptation can also help businesses to respond to changing consumer demands. As technology evolves, consumer preferences and behaviors change, and businesses need to adapt their offerings to meet these new demands. For example, the rise of e-commerce and mobile technology has led to changes in the way consumers shop, and businesses that have adapted to these changes have gained a competitive edge.

Another benefit of innovation and adaptation is that it can lead to cost savings and increased efficiency. By implementing new processes or technologies, businesses can streamline their operations and reduce waste, leading to cost savings and increased profitability. Additionally, innovation and adaptation can lead to new revenue streams, as businesses can identify new markets or customer segments that were previously untapped.

To identify opportunities for innovation and adaptation, businesses need to stay up-to-date on industry trends and consumer preferences. This requires constant research and analysis, as well as a willingness to take risks and experiment with new ideas. Businesses can also collaborate with other companies or experts in their industry to gain new perspectives and insights.

Examples of businesses that have successfully stayed ahead of the game through innovation and adaptation include Apple, Amazon, and Netflix. Apple revolutionized the smartphone industry with the introduction of the iPhone, and has continued to innovate with new products like the Apple Watch and AirPods. Amazon disrupted the traditional retail industry with its e-commerce platform and has continued to innovate with new services like Amazon Prime and Amazon Web Services. Netflix disrupted the entertainment industry with its streaming platform and has continued to innovate with original content and personalized recommendations.

In conclusion, innovation and adaptation are essential for businesses that want to stay ahead of the competition and achieve long-term success. By continuously evaluating their business and identifying opportunities for innovation, businesses can differentiate themselves, respond to changing consumer demands, and increase efficiency and profitability.

III. Building a Loyal Customer Base and Reputation

A strong and loyal customer base is essential for the long-term success of any business. A loyal customer base not only brings in repeat business but also acts as a brand ambassador, promoting your business through word of mouth. Building a positive reputation and a loyal customer base takes time, effort, and consistency. In this section, we will discuss some tips for building a loyal customer base and positive reputation, along with some examples of businesses that have successfully done so.

Tips for Building a Loyal Customer Base and Positive Reputation

1. **Offer Excellent Customer Service**: Customer service is one of the most critical aspects of building a loyal customer base. Ensure that your customers are always treated with respect and receive prompt and helpful responses to their inquiries or complaints.
2. **Build Personal Relationships with Your Customers**: Get to know your customers personally and show them that you care. Personalized communication and personalized services go a long way in building a loyal customer base.
3. **Provide High-Quality Products and Services**: Consistently provide high-quality products and services to your customers. This will build trust and establish your reputation as a reliable and reputable business.
4. **Be Transparent and Honest**: Honesty is always the best policy. Be transparent with your customers about your business operations and practices. This will help build trust and establish your reputation as an honest and trustworthy business.
5. **Stay Active on Social Media**: Social media is an excellent platform to connect with your customers and build relationships.

- Stay active on social media and engage with your customers through posts, comments, and messages.

Examples of Businesses that have Successfully Built a Loyal Customer Base and Positive Reputation

- **Apple**: Apple is known for its high-quality products and exceptional customer service. The company has built a loyal customer base by consistently providing innovative products and excellent customer service.
- **Amazon**: Amazon has built a loyal customer base by providing fast and reliable delivery, excellent customer service, and a wide selection of products at competitive prices.
- **Zappos**: Zappos has built a loyal customer base by providing exceptional customer service and a personalized shopping experience. The company offers free shipping and returns, along with a 365-day return policy, which has helped establish its reputation as a customer-centric business.

In conclusion, building a loyal customer base and positive reputation takes time and effort. By providing excellent customer service, building personal relationships with your customers, providing high-quality products and services, being transparent and honest, and staying active on social media, you can establish a loyal customer base and a positive reputation for your business.

IV. **Maintaining a Competitive Edge Through Continuous Learning and Improvement**

In today's rapidly changing business landscape, it is crucial to continuously learn and improve in order to stay ahead of the competition.

The benefits of continuous learning and improvement include increased efficiency, enhanced creativity, and improved customer satisfaction. This section will discuss the importance of continuous learning and improvement in business, provide tips for identifying areas for improvement, and offer examples of businesses that have successfully maintained a competitive edge through continuous learning and improvement.

Benefits of Continuous Learning and Improvement

Continuous learning and improvement are essential for maintaining a competitive edge in business. By continuously learning and improving, businesses can stay up-to-date with industry trends and customer preferences, identify areas for growth, and stay ahead of the competition. Some benefits of continuous learning and improvement include:

- **Increased Efficiency**: By continuously learning and improving, businesses can streamline their operations, reduce waste, and increase efficiency. This can result in cost savings, improved productivity, and increased profitability.
- **Enhanced Creativity**: Continuous learning and improvement can lead to enhanced creativity and innovation. By exposing themselves to new ideas and concepts, businesses can develop new products and services, improve existing ones, and differentiate themselves from the competition.
- **Improved Customer Satisfaction**: By continuously learning and improving, businesses can better meet the needs of their customers. This can result in improved customer satisfaction, increased customer loyalty, and a better reputation in the marketplace.

Tips for Identifying Areas for Improvement and Implementing Changes

Identifying areas for improvement and implementing changes can be a daunting task, but it is essential for maintaining a competitive edge. Here are some tips for identifying areas for improvement and implementing changes:

- **Gather Feedback**: Collect feedback from customers, employees, and other stakeholders to identify areas for improvement. This can be done through surveys, focus groups, or other forms of feedback.
- **Analyze Data:** Analyze data on sales, customer feedback, and other metrics to identify areas for improvement. Use this data to develop specific goals and action plans.
- **Stay Up-to-Date**: Stay up-to-date with industry trends and best practices to identify areas for improvement. Attend conferences, read industry publications, and participate in online forums to stay informed.
- **Experiment and Test**: Experiment with new ideas and test them on a small scale before implementing them company-wide. This can help identify potential issues and ensure that changes are effective.

Examples of Businesses That Have Successfully Maintained a Competitive Edge Through Continuous Learning and Improvement

Many successful businesses have maintained a competitive edge through continuous learning and improvement. One example is Amazon, which continuously experiments with new ideas and tests them on a small scale before implementing them company-wide. This has allowed Amazon to stay ahead of the competition and maintain its position as the world's largest online retailer.

Another example is Toyota, which has a culture of continuous improvement known as "Kaizen." Toyota employees are encouraged to identify areas for improvement and develop solutions to problems. This has helped Toyota maintain a competitive edge in the automotive industry and become one of the world's largest automakers.

In conclusion, maintaining a competitive edge through continuous learning and improvement is essential for long-term success in business. By continuously learning and improving, businesses can stay up-to-date with industry trends and customer preferences, identify areas for growth, and stay ahead of the competition. By gathering feedback, analyzing data, staying up-to-date, and experimenting with new ideas, businesses can identify areas for improvement and implement changes that lead to increased efficiency, enhanced creativity, and improved customer satisfaction.

V. Overcoming Challenges in Crushing Your Competition

Crushing your competition can be a challenging task, even with the right strategies and mindset. In this section, we will discuss some of the most common challenges businesses face when trying to crush their competition and how to overcome them.

1. **Lack of Differentiation**: One of the biggest challenges businesses face is a lack of differentiation. If your products or services are similar to your competitors', it can be hard to stand out and capture market share. To overcome this challenge, businesses need to focus on developing a unique value proposition that differentiates them from their competitors. This can involve investing in research and development, improving customer service, or offering a wider range of products or services.

- **Price Wars**: Competing on price is a common strategy for many businesses, but it can also be a race to the bottom. If you engage in a price war with your competitors, you may end up cutting your profits and damaging your brand's reputation. To overcome this challenge, businesses need to focus on offering value to their customers that goes beyond just price. This can involve offering better quality products or services, providing exceptional customer service, or offering unique features or benefits that competitors can't match.
- **Copycats**: Copycats are businesses that imitate your products or services, and may even try to replicate your marketing campaigns or branding. This can be frustrating for businesses that have invested a lot of time and resources into developing their products and brand. To overcome this challenge, businesses need to focus on building a strong brand identity that is difficult to replicate. This can involve investing in unique packaging, developing a strong social media presence, or using influencer marketing to build brand awareness.
- **Changing Market Trends**: Market trends can shift quickly, and businesses that fail to adapt may find themselves falling behind their competitors. To overcome this challenge, businesses need to stay informed about industry trends and be willing to pivot their strategies when necessary. This can involve investing in new technology, developing new products or services, or targeting new customer segments.

- **Negative Reviews**: In today's digital age, a single negative review can have a significant impact on a business's reputation. Negative reviews can damage a business's credibility and make it harder to attract new customers. To overcome this challenge, businesses need to focus on providing exceptional customer service and responding to negative reviews in a professional and constructive manner. This can involve offering refunds, apologizing for the inconvenience, or offering to make things right.

In conclusion, crushing your competition requires more than just having the right strategies and mindset. Businesses also need to be prepared to overcome the challenges they may face along the way. By focusing on differentiation, offering value beyond price, building a strong brand identity, staying informed about industry trends, and providing exceptional customer service, businesses can position themselves for long-term success in a competitive market.

VI. Conclusion

Chapter 8 of "Hustle Harder: How to Dominate the Game and Crush Your Competition" has covered a lot of ground when it comes to crushing your competition. We've discussed the importance of innovation, building a loyal customer base and positive reputation, maintaining a competitive edge through continuous learning and improvement, and overcoming challenges along the way.

Now, it's time to wrap up everything we've learned and provide you with some key takeaways to help you continue on your journey towards success.

Firstly, it's important to remember that crushing your competition is not about destroying them, but rather about improving your own business and striving towards excellence.

By focusing on innovation, you can create new products and services that set you apart from your competition and provide value to your customers.

Secondly, building a loyal customer base and positive reputation should be a top priority. Customers are the lifeblood of any business, and by treating them well and providing them with exceptional service, you can create a base of loyal customers who will keep coming back to you.

Thirdly, maintaining a competitive edge through continuous learning and improvement is critical. The business world is constantly changing, and staying up-to-date with the latest trends and technologies is essential to staying ahead of the competition.

Lastly, it's important to be aware of the challenges you may face along the way and be prepared to overcome them. Competition can be fierce, and it's important to stay focused on your own business and not get distracted by what others are doing.

In conclusion, crushing your competition is all about being the best version of yourself and striving for excellence in everything you do. By focusing on innovation, building a loyal customer base and positive reputation, maintaining a competitive edge through continuous learning and improvement, and overcoming challenges, you can position yourself for long-term success. Remember to stay focused, stay determined, and always keep hustling.

"Victory is always possible for the person who refuses to stop fighting."

- Napoleon Hill

Chapter 9: Maintaining Work-Life Balance

I. **Introduction**
   - Explanation of the importance of maintaining work-life balance for entrepreneurs
   - Overview of the topics to be covered in the chapter

II. **Avoiding burnout and managing stress**
   - Discussion of the negative effects of burnout and chronic stress on business success and personal well-being
   - Tips for recognizing signs of burnout and stress and taking action to prevent them
   - Strategies for managing stress, including time management, delegation, and mindfulness techniques

III. **Prioritizing self-care and personal growth**
   - Explanation of the importance of self-care and personal growth for entrepreneurs
   - Tips for developing a self-care routine, including exercise, nutrition, and rest
   - Strategies for personal growth and development, including reading, networking, and learning new skills

IV. **Creating a fulfilling and sustainable lifestyle as an entrepreneur**
   - Discussion of the challenges of balancing work and personal life as an entrepreneur
   - Tips for creating a schedule and routine that prioritizes personal time and relationships
   - Strategies for finding fulfillment and meaning outside of work, including hobbies, volunteering, and travel

V. Conclusion
- Recap of key points and strategies for maintaining work-life balance as an entrepreneur
- Encouragement to prioritize self-care and personal growth for long-term success
- Final thoughts from the author on the importance of balancing work and personal life for overall success.

Chapter 9: Maintaining Work-Life Balance

I. Introduction

As an entrepreneur, it can be easy to become consumed by the demands of running a business. However, it's essential to maintain a healthy work-life balance in order to avoid burnout and maintain long-term success.

Maintaining work-life balance involves finding a way to juggle the responsibilities of your business with your personal life, hobbies, and interests. It's about creating boundaries and making time for the things that matter most to you outside of work.

There are many benefits to maintaining work-life balance as an entrepreneur. It can help reduce stress, improve relationships with loved ones, increase productivity, and ultimately lead to greater success in both your personal and professional life.

In this chapter, we will explore strategies for avoiding burnout and managing stress, prioritizing self-care and personal growth, and creating a fulfilling and sustainable lifestyle as an entrepreneur. By implementing these strategies, you can achieve a healthier work-life balance and maintain long-term success in your business.

II. Avoiding burnout and managing stress

As an entrepreneur, it is common to feel like you have to hustle non-stop to succeed. While hard work is important, it is equally important to take care of yourself and avoid burnout. Burnout is a state of emotional, physical, and mental exhaustion caused by excessive and prolonged stress.

It can lead to a decrease in productivity, motivation, and creativity, and can negatively impact your health and well-being. In this section, we will discuss the negative effects of burnout and chronic stress, as well as provide tips and strategies for avoiding burnout and managing stress.

One of the negative effects of burnout is a decrease in productivity. When you are burnt out, it is difficult to focus and complete tasks efficiently. This can lead to missed deadlines and a decline in the quality of your work. Burnout can also lead to a decrease in motivation, which can make it difficult to stay committed to your business goals. Chronic stress can also negatively affect your physical health. It can lead to headaches, muscle tension, and fatigue, among other symptoms. Over time, chronic stress can increase your risk of developing certain health conditions, such as heart disease and diabetes.

To avoid burnout and manage stress, it is important to recognize the signs and take action. Some common signs of burnout include feeling exhausted all the time, losing interest in your work, and becoming easily irritated or frustrated. If you are experiencing any of these symptoms, it is important to take a step back and assess the situation. Ask yourself what is causing the stress and how you can reduce it. Some strategies for managing stress include practicing good time management, delegating tasks to others, and engaging in mindfulness techniques such as meditation and deep breathing exercises.

One important strategy for avoiding burnout and managing stress is to prioritize self-care. This means taking care of your physical, mental, and emotional well-being. Make sure to get enough sleep, eat a healthy diet, and exercise regularly. Engage in activities that bring you joy and relaxation, such as spending time with loved ones or pursuing a hobby.

It is also important to set boundaries and learn to say no when you need to. This can help prevent you from overcommitting and feeling overwhelmed.

In conclusion, avoiding burnout and managing stress is essential for maintaining work-life balance as an entrepreneur. Burnout can have negative effects on your business and personal well-being, but with proper self-care and stress management techniques, it can be avoided. By recognizing the signs of burnout, prioritizing self-care, and using effective stress management strategies, you can maintain a fulfilling and sustainable lifestyle as an entrepreneur.

III. **Prioritizing self-care and personal growth**

Entrepreneurship can be a demanding and challenging journey, with long hours, intense pressure, and constant decision-making. While it's essential to focus on your business's success, it's equally important to prioritize your own well-being and personal growth. Self-care and personal growth are critical to maintaining a healthy work-life balance and achieving long-term success as an entrepreneur.

Self-care involves taking care of your physical, mental, and emotional health. It includes basic practices such as getting enough sleep, eating healthy food, and exercising regularly. These practices might seem simple, but they can make a significant difference in your energy levels, mood, and overall well-being. For instance, getting enough sleep can help you stay focused and productive, while regular exercise can reduce stress and anxiety.

Aside from basic self-care practices, entrepreneurs can also benefit from developing a self-care routine that fits their unique needs and preferences.

This routine can include activities that help you relax and recharge, such as meditation, yoga, or a hobby that you enjoy. It's essential to make time for these activities regularly, even if it means scheduling them into your busy day.

Personal growth and development are also crucial for entrepreneurs. As your business grows and evolves, it's essential to continue learning and developing your skills and knowledge. This can involve reading books or articles on business, attending workshops or seminars, or networking with other entrepreneurs in your industry.

Continuing education can help you stay ahead of the curve and adapt to new trends and technologies in your industry. It can also give you new perspectives and insights that you can apply to your business. Networking with other entrepreneurs can also provide valuable support, advice, and potential partnerships that can help you grow your business.

In conclusion, prioritizing self-care and personal growth is critical for maintaining a healthy work-life balance and achieving long-term success as an entrepreneur. By taking care of your physical, mental, and emotional health and continuing to learn and develop your skills, you can build a fulfilling and sustainable lifestyle as an entrepreneur.

IV. Creating a Fulfilling and Sustainable Lifestyle as an Entrepreneur

Entrepreneurship can be a fulfilling and rewarding experience, but it can also be challenging to balance work and personal life. Many entrepreneurs struggle to find time for themselves, their families, and their personal interests while working to build and grow their businesses. However, creating a fulfilling and sustainable lifestyle is crucial for long-term success and well-being.

One of the key challenges of being an entrepreneur is the constant pressure to work long hours and stay connected to the business at all times. This can lead to burnout and a lack of balance in life. To create a fulfilling and sustainable lifestyle, it's essential to establish a schedule and routine that prioritizes personal time and relationships.

Start by identifying your most important personal priorities, such as spending time with family and friends, pursuing hobbies and interests, or taking care of your health. Then, create a schedule that allocates time for these activities and stick to it as much as possible. This will help ensure that you have time for the things that matter most to you, even as you work to grow your business.

Another important aspect of creating a fulfilling and sustainable lifestyle is finding ways to create meaning and fulfillment outside of work. Many entrepreneurs derive a sense of purpose and identity from their businesses, but it's important to have other sources of meaning and fulfillment as well. This might include volunteering for a cause you care about, traveling to new places, or pursuing a creative hobby.

In addition to these strategies, it's important to practice self-care and take care of your physical and mental health. This might include exercise, healthy eating, getting enough sleep, and taking breaks from work to relax and recharge. It's also important to find ways to manage stress, such as mindfulness techniques or working with a coach or therapist.

Finally, it's essential to recognize that creating a fulfilling and sustainable lifestyle is an ongoing process. As your business grows and evolves, your personal priorities and needs may change as well. It's important to remain flexible and adaptable, and to continually reassess your priorities and adjust your schedule and routine as needed.

In conclusion, creating a fulfilling and sustainable lifestyle as an entrepreneur is essential for long-term success and well-being. By prioritizing personal time and relationships, finding sources of meaning and fulfillment outside of work, and practicing self-care, entrepreneurs can build a life that is both rewarding and sustainable.

V. Conclusion

Recap of Key Points and Strategies for Maintaining Work-Life Balance as an Entrepreneur

In this chapter, we've explored the challenges of maintaining a healthy work-life balance as an entrepreneur and the importance of doing so. We've discussed several strategies that can help you achieve this balance, including:

- **Setting clear boundaries**: Be intentional about when you work and when you don't. Create a schedule and stick to it as much as possible.
- **Prioritizing your time**: Focus on the tasks that are most important and delegate or outsource others as needed. Use time-blocking to manage your schedule and avoid distractions.
- **Taking care of yourself**: Make time for exercise, healthy eating, and self-care activities that help you recharge and reduce stress.
- **Making time for loved ones**: Schedule regular time with family and friends to maintain healthy relationships and avoid burnout.
- **Finding ways to disconnect**: Set aside time each day to disconnect from work and technology, whether it's through meditation, reading, or other hobbies you enjoy.

Encouragement to Prioritize Self-Care and Personal Growth for Long-Term Success

It's easy to get caught up in the day-to-day tasks of running a business and forget about the importance of self-care and personal growth. However, neglecting these areas can have long-term consequences for your health, happiness, and success.

Make self-care a priority by scheduling time for exercise, healthy eating, and relaxation. This can help reduce stress, improve mental clarity, and increase productivity.

Additionally, make time for activities that bring you joy, such as reading, painting, or playing music.

Personal growth is also essential for long-term success. This means taking the time to learn new skills, develop new interests, and challenge yourself. It can be helpful to set goals for yourself in both your personal and professional life and work towards achieving them.

Final Thoughts from the Author on the Importance of Balancing Work and Personal Life for Overall Success

Maintaining a healthy work-life balance is not just about achieving short-term goals or avoiding burnout. It's about creating a sustainable lifestyle that supports your long-term success and happiness.

As an entrepreneur, it can be challenging to balance the demands of running a business with your personal life. However, it's crucial to find ways to disconnect from work, prioritize self-care and personal growth, and make time for loved ones.

By implementing the strategies discussed in this chapter and making work-life balance a priority, you can achieve greater success in both your personal and professional life. Remember, success is not just about what you achieve in business, but also about how you live your life.

"If you want to change the world, go home and love your family."

- Mother Teresa

Chapter 10: Conclusion: The Hustle Never Ends

I. **Introduction**
   - Recap of the book's main themes and ideas
   - Brief summary of Chapter 10's content

II. **Recap of key lessons and takeaways**
   - Review of the most important lessons and takeaways from the book
   - Emphasis on the importance of hard work, perseverance, and a growth mindset

III. **Encouragement to keep hustling and pursuing your dreams**
   - Motivational messages to inspire readers to keep working hard and chasing their goals
   - Examples of successful entrepreneurs who have overcome challenges and achieved success through hard work and persistence

IV. **Final thoughts and inspiration to keep pushing forward**
   - Reflections on the author's personal journey and experiences
   - Encouragement to continue learning, growing, and pushing oneself to reach new heights
   - Final words of inspiration and motivation to keep hustling and never give up on one's dreams

V. **Conclusion**
   - Recap of the key points covered in Chapter 10
   - Final message of encouragement and inspiration to readers

Chapter 10: Conclusion: The Hustle Never Ends

I. Introduction

As we come to the end of this book, it's important to reflect on the main themes and ideas that have been presented throughout its pages. From the importance of setting clear goals and having a strong work ethic to the need for adaptability and resilience, Hustle Harder has provided a comprehensive guide for anyone looking to dominate their industry and crush their competition.

In this final chapter, we'll take a closer look at the key takeaways from the book as a whole, and we'll summarize the main points covered in Chapter 10.

Brief Summary of Chapter 10's Content

Chapter 10 serves as a call to action for readers, reminding them that the hustle never truly ends. While it's important to take time to celebrate your successes and recharge your batteries, there is always more work to be done if you want to stay on top.

One of the main themes of Chapter 10 is the importance of staying hungry and motivated. Whether you've already achieved significant success or you're just starting out, it's crucial to maintain a sense of drive and ambition. This means setting new goals, challenging yourself to push beyond your limits, and constantly seeking out opportunities to learn and grow.

Another key point in this chapter is the idea that failure is an inevitable part of the journey to success. No matter how talented or hardworking you are, you're bound to face setbacks and obstacles along the way.

The key is to view these challenges as opportunities for growth and learning, rather than as roadblocks that will stop you in your tracks

Finally, Chapter 10 emphasizes the importance of resilience and perseverance. The road to success is rarely easy, and there will be times when you feel like giving up. But it's in these moments that your true character is revealed. By staying committed to your goals, even when the going gets tough, you'll build the mental and emotional resilience you need to weather any storm.

Conclusion

As we wrap up this book, I hope you feel inspired and empowered to take your hustle to the next level. Remember, the journey to success is a marathon, not a sprint. It requires dedication, hard work, and a willingness to push through even when things get tough.

But with the right mindset and the strategies outlined in this book, you can dominate your industry and crush your competition. So keep hustling, keep pushing yourself to be better, and never forget that the only limit to your success is the one you set for yourself.

II. **Recap of key lessons and takeaways**

As we come to the end of this book, it's important to reflect on the key lessons and takeaways that we've covered throughout the chapters. One of the most important themes that runs through the book is the importance of hard work, perseverance, and a growth mindset. These qualities are essential for anyone who wants to succeed in today's competitive business world.

One of the main messages of this book is that success is not a matter of luck or innate talent, but rather the result of consistent effort and a willingness to learn and grow.

This means that if you want to achieve your goals and dominate your competition, you need to be willing to put in the hard work and make the necessary sacrifices.

Another key lesson from this book is the importance of taking risks and stepping outside of your comfort zone. Many of the most successful entrepreneurs and business leaders have achieved their success by taking bold, calculated risks and seizing opportunities when they arise. This requires a certain level of confidence and self-belief, as well as the willingness to learn from your failures and keep pushing forward.

In addition to these lessons, the book also emphasizes the importance of staying focused and disciplined, setting clear goals and priorities, and building strong relationships with your customers, employees, and business partners. These are all essential qualities for anyone who wants to build a successful and sustainable business over the long term.

Ultimately, the key takeaway from this book is that success is not something that can be achieved overnight, but rather the result of a long-term commitment to hard work, growth, and learning. By adopting a growth mindset and embracing the principles and strategies outlined in this book, you can position yourself for success and achieve your goals, no matter what challenges you may face along the way.

In conclusion, the lessons and takeaways from this book are more relevant and important than ever before, as we continue to navigate an increasingly complex and competitive business landscape. By staying focused on the principles of hard work, perseverance, and a growth mindset, you can build a successful and fulfilling career, and make a positive impact in the world around you. So keep hustling, keep learning, and never give up on your dreams!

III. Encouragement to keep hustling and pursuing your dreams

In the previous chapter, we discussed the importance of continuing to hustle and grind even after achieving some level of success. The journey of an entrepreneur is never-ending, and there is always room for growth and improvement. It is important to remain hungry and motivated to pursue your dreams and achieve your goals.

One of the most significant factors that contribute to success is having a growth mindset. The idea that your abilities and intelligence can be developed through hard work, dedication, and perseverance is what separates successful entrepreneurs from those who give up at the first sign of failure. As an entrepreneur, you must embrace challenges as opportunities for growth and development.

There will always be obstacles and roadblocks on your entrepreneurial journey, but it's important to stay committed and focused on your goals. It's easy to get discouraged and lose motivation when faced with setbacks, but successful entrepreneurs understand that failure is an essential part of the learning process. It's crucial to keep a positive attitude, stay persistent, and keep hustling towards your dreams.

One way to stay motivated is by setting achievable goals. These goals should be specific, measurable, achievable, relevant, and time-bound. By setting these goals, you can track your progress and stay motivated to achieve them. Celebrate your small wins and use them as fuel to keep pushing forward.

Another way to stay motivated is by surrounding yourself with like-minded individuals. Join entrepreneurial communities, attend networking events, and connect with other entrepreneurs who share your vision and values. These connections can provide support, motivation, and inspiration, and can help you overcome obstacles and achieve success.

There are numerous examples of successful entrepreneurs who have overcome challenges and achieved success through hard work and persistence. Take Oprah Winfrey, for example. She started her career as a news anchor and worked her way up to become one of the most successful media moguls in the world. Despite facing discrimination and setbacks throughout her career, she remained focused on her goals and persevered through adversity. Her story is a testament to the power of hard work and determination.

In conclusion, entrepreneurship is a never-ending journey that requires hard work, dedication, and perseverance. The road to success is never easy, but with a growth mindset and a commitment to pursuing your dreams, anything is possible. Stay focused, set achievable goals, surround yourself with like-minded individuals, and remain hungry for success. Remember that failure is an essential part of the learning process, and it's essential to stay persistent and keep hustling towards your dreams.

IV. **Final thoughts and inspiration to keep pushing forward**

As I reflect on my personal journey and experiences, I am reminded of the countless obstacles and challenges that I have faced as an entrepreneur. From the early days of hustling on the streets to the present day of running a successful business, I have learned that the hustle never truly ends.

But it is this very mindset that has allowed me to push forward, to continue learning and growing, and to pursue my dreams with unwavering determination. And it is this same mindset that I hope to instill in my readers as they embark on their own entrepreneurial journeys.

No matter where you are in your career, I encourage you to keep pushing yourself to reach new heights.

Set ambitious goals, take calculated risks, and don't be afraid to fail. Remember, failure is not the opposite of success, it is simply a stepping stone on the path to success.

But even as you strive for greatness, don't forget to enjoy the journey. Take time to celebrate your wins, no matter how small they may seem, and never lose sight of what truly matters in life. Whether it's spending time with loved ones, pursuing hobbies and passions, or simply taking a moment to appreciate the beauty of the world around us, it is these moments that make life truly fulfilling.

So, as I close this book, I leave you with these final words of inspiration and motivation: keep hustling, keep pushing yourself to be the best you can be, and never give up on your dreams. With hard work, perseverance, and a growth mindset, anything is possible.

V. Conclusion

As we come to the end of this book, I want to take a moment to reflect on the key points we covered in Chapter 10 and offer a final message of encouragement and inspiration to all of my readers.

Throughout this chapter, we discussed the importance of never giving up on our dreams and continuing to hustle even when faced with obstacles and challenges. We reviewed some of the most important lessons and takeaways from the book, including the importance of hard work, perseverance, and a growth mindset. We also explored the stories of successful entrepreneurs who overcame adversity through hard work and persistence, and discussed the importance of learning, growing, and pushing ourselves to reach new heights.

In reflecting on my personal journey and experiences, I want to remind you that success is not a destination, but rather a continuous journey.

There will always be new challenges to face and new opportunities to pursue. But with a strong work ethic, a never-give-up attitude, and a commitment to personal growth, you can achieve anything you set your mind to. So, my final message to you is this: keep hustling, keep pushing yourself, and never lose sight of your dreams. Remember that every setback is an opportunity to learn and grow, and that every success is a chance to set your sights even higher. With the right mindset and the determination to succeed, anything is possible.

Thank you for joining me on this journey. I wish you all the best in your own pursuits, and I hope that the lessons and insights shared in this book will help you to dominate the game and crush your competition. The hustle never ends, so let's keep pushing forward together.

"Success is not how high you have climbed, but how you make a positive difference to the world."

- Roy T. Bennett

Epilogue: The Bonus Chapter

I. **Introduction**
- Explanation of the purpose of the bonus chapter
- Brief summary of what readers can expect to find in the chapter

II. **Few insights**
- Discussion of a few additional insights or tips related to hustling and achieving success
- Examples of successful entrepreneurs who have applied these insights in their own careers

III. **Tasks to start hustling**
- Specific tasks or exercises assigned to readers to help them get started on their own hustle journey
- Emphasis on the importance of taking action and putting in the work

IV. **Questions to find your ideal hustle**
- A set of questions for readers to answer that will help them identify their passions and strengths
- Guidance on how to use this information to find their ideal hustle or business venture

V. **Conclusion**
- Final words of encouragement and inspiration to keep hustling and pursuing one's dreams
- Reminder of the key takeaways from the book and how they can be applied to readers' own lives and careers

Epilogue: The Bonus Chapter

As we come to the end of this book, I wanted to leave readers with some additional insights and tasks to help them continue their journey towards success. This bonus chapter is designed to provide a little extra motivation and guidance for those who are ready to take their hustle to the next level.

The purpose of this chapter is to encourage readers to start taking action towards their goals, rather than just reading about them. It's easy to get caught up in the theory of success, but true success comes from putting that theory into practice. In this chapter, you will find a few additional insights and actionable steps to help you start hustling harder than ever before.

First and foremost, it's important to recognize that success is not a one-size-fits-all solution. Each person's journey towards success will be unique, and what works for one person may not work for another. That's why it's important to take the time to find your ideal hustle, the path that aligns with your skills, passions, and values.

To help you on this journey, I have included a series of questions for you to consider. These questions are designed to help you reflect on your strengths, weaknesses, and aspirations, and to identify the opportunities that are available to you. By answering these questions honestly and thoughtfully, you will gain a better understanding of yourself and what you need to do to achieve your goals.

In addition to these questions, I have also included a series of tasks to help you get started on your hustle. These tasks are designed to be actionable steps that you can take today to start moving towards your goals.

Whether it's reaching out to a potential mentor, starting a side hustle, or simply practicing a new skill, these tasks are meant to help you build momentum and gain confidence in your ability to succeed.

As you embark on this new journey, it's important to remember that success is not a destination, but a process. There will be ups and downs along the way, but it's important to stay focused on your goals and keep hustling harder than ever before. With the insights and tasks in this bonus chapter, you have everything you need to start taking action towards your dreams.

In conclusion, I hope that this book has provided you with the inspiration, motivation, and guidance you need to start hustling harder and dominating the game. Remember, success is within your reach, but it requires hard work, perseverance, and a growth mindset. Keep pushing yourself to be the best you can be, and never give up on your dreams. The hustle never ends, but with the right mindset and tools, you can achieve anything you set your mind to.

Welcome to the bonus chapter of Hustle Harder: How to Dominate the Game and Crush Your Competition. This chapter provides a few additional insights and tips related to hustling and achieving success, which can further help you to grow and achieve your goals.

As you may know, hustling is not just about working hard, but it is also about working smart. In this chapter, we will discuss a few insights and tips that can help you to maximize your potential and achieve greater success in your life.

One of the most important insights for hustling is to always stay focused on your goals. It is easy to get distracted by the day-to-day tasks, but it is important to keep your eye on the prize.

Focus on your long-term goals and create a roadmap to achieve them. Once you have a clear vision of your goals, break them down into smaller achievable steps. Each step you take brings you closer to achieving your ultimate goal.

Another important insight is to surround yourself with positive and supportive people. It is said that we become the average of the people we spend the most time with, so it is crucial to surround yourself with people who inspire and motivate you to achieve your goals. Find mentors or people in your industry who have achieved the level of success that you aspire to, and learn from them. They can provide you with valuable insights and advice to help you grow and succeed.

In addition to these insights, it is also important to constantly learn and develop new skills. As the world changes, so does the industry you are in. It is important to keep up with the latest trends and technologies to stay relevant and ahead of the game. Attend conferences, take online courses, and read books related to your industry to keep up with the latest developments.

Finally, always stay hungry for success. Don't get complacent and never stop hustling. Remember that there is always more to achieve, and the only limit to your success is your own mindset. Keep pushing yourself to reach new heights and never settle for anything less than your best.

To wrap up, the key takeaway from this chapter is to always stay focused on your goals, surround yourself with positive and supportive people, constantly learn and develop new skills, and always stay hungry for success. By applying these insights and tips, you can maximize your potential and achieve greater success in your life.

Congratulations on finishing the book, "Hustle Harder: How to Dominate the Game and Crush Your Competition!" By now, you have learned a lot about what it takes to become a successful entrepreneur and achieve your dreams. However, the real challenge comes in putting that knowledge into action. In this bonus chapter, I have included some specific tasks and exercises that I encourage you to complete in order to help you get started on your own hustle journey. These tasks will help you take the ideas and concepts presented in the book and turn them into actionable steps that you can apply to your own life.

Task 1: Define your goals

The first step in any journey is to define your destination. In order to start hustling, you need to have a clear understanding of what you want to achieve. Take some time to think about your long-term goals and write them down. Be specific about what you want to achieve and by when. Once you have a clear picture of your goals, you can start to work towards them.

Task 2: Develop a plan

Now that you know where you want to go, it's time to develop a plan for getting there. Break down your long-term goals into smaller, more manageable steps. Create a timeline for achieving each step and be sure to include milestones along the way to help you stay motivated.

Task 3: Take action

The most important part of any plan is taking action. Without action, your plan is just a list of ideas. Start taking small steps towards your goals every day. Celebrate your successes and learn from your failures. Remember, the journey to success is not a straight line. There will be bumps along the way, but the important thing is to keep moving forward.

Task 4: Get uncomfortable

If you want to achieve success, you need to be willing to get uncomfortable.

This means taking risks and stepping outside of your comfort zone. Don't be afraid to try new things and take on new challenges. Push yourself to do things that scare you, because that's where growth happens.

Task 5: Surround yourself with like-minded people

Finally, surround yourself with people who share your values and goals. Seek out mentors and colleagues who can provide guidance and support. Join networking groups and attend events where you can meet other entrepreneurs and business professionals. The people you surround yourself with will have a big impact on your success, so choose wisely.

In conclusion, I encourage you to take these tasks seriously and make them a priority. Remember, the most important part of any journey is taking the first step. Don't be afraid to make mistakes or fail along the way. The key is to keep hustling and never give up on your dreams. Good luck on your journey, and I wish you all the success in the world!

In the previous chapter, we talked about the importance of taking action and putting in the work to achieve success in your chosen field. But what if you're not quite sure what that field should be? How do you identify your passions and strengths, and use that information to find your ideal hustle or business venture? In this section, we'll explore a set of questions that can help you do just that.

What are your hobbies and interests?

Think about the things you enjoy doing in your free time. What hobbies or interests do you have? Are there any topics or activities that you could spend hours talking about or reading about without getting bored? Your hobbies and interests can often provide clues to your passions and strengths.

What are your values?
Your values are the principles or beliefs that are most important to you. For example, you might value honesty, integrity, hard work, or creativity. Think about your values and how they align with different career paths. Are there certain industries or roles that would allow you to live according to your values?

What are your natural talents and abilities?
Consider the things that come easily to you. Maybe you're a great communicator, or you have a talent for graphic design. These natural talents and abilities can be a good indication of the areas where you're most likely to excel.

What problems do you enjoy solving?
Think about the types of problems that you enjoy solving. Maybe you're great at troubleshooting technical issues, or you have a knack for resolving conflicts. Identifying the types of problems that you enjoy solving can help you identify potential career paths or business ideas.

What are your goals?
What are you hoping to achieve in your life and career? Are there certain accomplishments or milestones that you're working towards? Your goals can provide direction and focus as you explore different career paths or business ventures.

Once you've answered these questions, take some time to reflect on your answers. Look for patterns or themes that emerge. For example, maybe you've identified a few different hobbies or interests that all relate to marketing, or maybe you've realized that your values align with a certain type of business or industry.

Use this information to start exploring different career paths or business ideas. Look for opportunities to learn and grow in areas that align with your passions and strengths. Don't be afraid to take risks and try new things.

Remember, the hustle never ends, but with the right mindset and approach, you can build a successful and fulfilling career doing something that you love.

Congratulations on making it to the end of Hustle Harder! By now, you should have gained a deeper understanding of what it takes to succeed in the game and crush your competition. But this is just the beginning. The real work starts now as you put the principles and strategies outlined in this book into action.

I want to leave you with some final words of encouragement and inspiration to keep hustling and pursuing your dreams.

Remember that success is not a destination but a journey. It's not something that you achieve and then forget about. It's a continuous process of growth, learning, and improvement.

Here are some key takeaways from the book and how you can apply them to your own life and career:

Hustle Harder

The first and most important lesson of this book is that you need to hustle harder than anyone else if you want to succeed. Hustle is not just about working harder, but also about working smarter. It's about being strategic, focused, and relentless in the pursuit of your goals. So, whatever your dream may be, don't just sit around waiting for it to happen. Go out there and make it happen.

Build Your Personal Brand

In today's world, your personal brand is everything. It's how you differentiate yourself from others and how you create a lasting impression in people's minds. Building a strong personal brand requires consistency, authenticity, and a clear understanding of your values and goals. So, take some time to define your personal brand and make sure that everything you do aligns with it.

Embrace Failure

Failure is not something to be ashamed of; it's a natural part of the learning process. In fact, some of the most successful people in the world have failed countless times before achieving their goals. So, don't be afraid to take risks and make mistakes. Use failure as an opportunity to learn and grow, and don't let it discourage you from pursuing your dreams.

Focus on Your Strengths

One of the biggest mistakes that people make is trying to be good at everything. The truth is, no one is good at everything, and you don't need to be. Instead, focus on your strengths and find ways to leverage them to achieve your goals. This will not only make you more successful but also more fulfilled and happy in your career.

Surround Yourself with Like-Minded People

Success is not a solo journey; it's a team sport. Surrounding yourself with like-minded people who share your values and goals is one of the most important things you can do to achieve success. These people will not only inspire and motivate you but also hold you accountable and provide valuable feedback.

In conclusion, Hustle Harder is not just a book; it's a philosophy and a way of life. By embracing the principles and strategies outlined in this book, you can achieve anything you set your mind to. So, keep hustling, keep grinding, and never give up on your dreams. Remember, the only limit to what you can achieve is the limit you set for yourself.

Dear Reader,

Thank you for taking the time to read "Hustle Harder: How to Dominate the Game and Crush Your Competition". I hope that you have found the book informative, engaging, and most importantly, empowering.

This book was written with the intention of motivating you to take control of your life and become the best version of yourself. I understand that the road to success can be challenging, but I believe that with the right mindset and a strong work ethic, you can achieve anything you set your mind to.

Throughout the chapters, I have shared practical strategies and advice on how to navigate the competitive landscape of business and entrepreneurship. I have also included inspiring stories of individuals who have overcome obstacles and achieved great success through hard work and determination.

My hope is that you have gained valuable insights and inspiration from this book, and that you will use them to fuel your own journey towards success. Remember, the road may be tough, but the rewards are worth it.

Thank you again for choosing "Hustle Harder: How to Dominate the Game and Crush Your Competition". I wish you all the best on your journey.

Sincerely,
Vinit Saraogi

"Success is not final, failure is not fatal: It is the courage to continue that counts."

- Winston Churchill

www.ingramcontent.com/pod-product-compliance
Lightning Source LLC
Chambersburg PA
CBHW031628210526
45464CB00004B/1-03